HIKE
MOJAVE NATIONAL PRESERVE

Hike. Contemplate what makes you happy and what makes you happier still. Follow a trail or blaze a new one. **Hike**. Think about what you can do to expand your life and someone else's. **Hike**. Slow down. Gear up. **Hike**. Connect with friends. Re-connect with nature.

Hike. Shed stress. Feel blessed. **Hike** to remember. **Hike** to forget. **Hike** for recovery. **Hike** for discovery. **Hike**. Enjoy the beauty of providence. **Hike**. Share the way, The Hiker's Way, on the long and winding trail we call life.

HIKE MOJAVE NATIONAL PRESERVE

BY
JOHN MCKINNEY

TheTrailmaster.com

HIKE Mojave National Preserve By John McKinney

HIKE Mojave National Preserve © 2022 The Trailmaster, Inc. All rights reserved. No part of this book may be used or reproduced in any manner whatsoever without written permission except in the case of brief quotations embodied in articles and reviews.

Layout and e-book by Lisa DeSpain
Cartography by Mark Chumley
HIKE Series Editor: Cheri Rae

Published by Olympus Press and The Trailmaster, Inc. www.TheTrailmaster.com (Visit our site for a complete listing of all Trailmaster publications, products, and services.)

Although The Trailmaster, Inc. and the author have made every attempt to ensure that information in this book is accurate, they are not responsible for any loss, damage, injury, or inconvenience that may occur to you while using this information. You are responsible for your own safety; the fact that an activity or trail is described in this book does not mean it will be safe for you. Trail conditions can change from day to day; always check local conditions and know your limitations.

Contents

Introduction 9

Mojave National Preserve 16

I Off I-15

Afton Canyon 25
    Along the Mojave River and "Grand Canyon of the Mojave"

Zzyzx 29
    Soda Springs, Doc Springer and Lake Tuendae Nature Trail

Clark Mountain 33
    Fir Canyon and MNP's highest summit

II Kelbaker Road & Heart of the Preserve

Kelbaker Hills 39
    Close-to-the-paved road wilderness experience

Lava Beds 43
    Go with the flow in MNP's northern lava beds

Lava Tube & Cinder Cones 47
    Go lava-tubing, climb a cinder cone, walk a moonscape

Kelso Depot Visitor Center 51
    Stop for a walk and ranger talk and MNP's major visitor center

Kelso Dunes 55
   Magnificent and booming dunes, some of America's tallest

Granite Mountains 59
   Summit Silver Peak for vistas of MNP's most famed features

Rock Spring 63
   From Rock House to watering hole to old Army Outpost

Hole-in-the-Wall 67
   Unforgettable! Iron rings aid descent into a twisted maze of volcanic rock.

Hole-in-the-Wall Nature Trail 71
   ID desert plants on short nature trail

Barber Peak 73
   Loop around mesa from Hole-in-the-Wall to Opalite Cliffs

Mid Hills to Hole-in-the-Wall 77
   Centerpieces of preserve linked by its longest and best trail

III Providence Mountains

Mitchell Caverns 83
   The Great Indoors: underground tour of dramatic limestone caves

Providence Mountains 87
   Through Crystal Spring Canyon to 100-mile vistas

Mary Beal's Mojave 91
   Nature Trail offers great introduction to high desert flora

IV Ivanpah Valley

CIMA DOME & TEUTONIA PEAK 95
    From the world's largest Joshua tree forest to Teutonia Peak

NIPTON 99
    Historic town and gateway community to MNP

V New York Mountains

CARUTHERS CANYON 103
    What's a coastal ecosystem doing in the middle of the desert?

KEYSTONE CANYON & NEW YORK PEAK 107
    Isolated community of pinyon pine and white fir

VI Off Route 66

PIUTE CANYON 113
    Fort Piute, magnificent Piute Gorge, and Old Mojave Road

AMBOY CRATER 117
    Hike a volcano near best-preserved stretch of old Route 66

MOJAVE NATIONAL PRESERVE STORIES 120

CALIFORNIA'S NATIONAL PARKS 131

ABOUT THE AUTHOR 142

*Hike the Kelso Dunes, one highlight of
"the Crown Jewel of the California Desert."*

EVERY TRAIL TELLS A STORY.

Introduction

Mojave National Preserve beckons the hiker with singing sand dunes, the world's largest Joshua tree forest and a dozen mountain ranges. The preserve boasts a wonderful concentration of mining history, tabletop mesas, cinder cones, back roads and footpaths. It has great diversity: everything that makes a desert a desert.

What Mojave National Preserve doesn't have is many visitors.

To many travelers, the Mojave is that vast, bleak, and seemingly interminable stretch of desert to be crossed as quickly as possible while driving Interstate 15 from Barstow to Las Vegas. Few realize that I-15 is the northern boundary of what desert rats have long called "the Crown Jewel of the California Desert."

Some 17 million people live less than a four-hour's drive from Mojave National Preserve but few city dwellers can locate this desert land on the map. Compared to its sister national parks—Death Valley and Joshua Tree, with annual visitation measured in the millions—MNP is far less traveled and even now, nearly 30 years after its creation, is still very much "The Lonesome Triangle."

What company you'll find will be good company—at least from the hiker's point of view. According to a National Park Service survey, half of all visitors say they come to Mojave for nature study and hiking. Visitation will increase as word of MNP's attractions spreads across the nation and around the world.

And it will be hikers who spread the word.

My small contribution to this desert land's preservation was in spreading the word. In the late 1980s, the Sierra Club and other conservationists were in heated battle with off-roaders and miners over the fate of the

Before the Preserve, all signs pointed to East Mojave National Scenic Area

eastern Mojave; the U.S. Bureau of Land Management, the agency in charge, was caught in the crossfire.

On a press junket to Kelso Dunes, after listening to all these interest groups argue with each other about this land, author Cheri Rae and I had an ah-ha moment: The public—and decision-makers in Washington—were getting left out of the discussion and had no idea about the features of this grand landscape or clue why it might be worthy of national park status.

Cheri and I got right to work and wrote and published a guidebook, *East Mojave National Scenic Area: A Visitors Guide*. And we literally put the Mojave on the map—producing a big map with all the area highlights. With those resources in hand, the public and politicians could more easily understand what was out

The vast desert wonderland, Mojave National Preserve, was created in 1994.

there and make the right decision. We were pleased when Congress passed the California Desert Protection Act in 1994 that created Mojave National Preserve and made the National Park Service its steward.

Everywhere in this vast 1.6-million-acre national parkland are mountain ranges, small and large, from the jagged, spire-like Castle Peaks to flat-topped Table Mountain. In fact, despite evidence to the contrary—notably the stunning Kelso Dunes—MNP is really a desert of mountains not sand.

Mountainous the Mojave may be, but with that being said, by far the most popular hike in the preserve is the trail-less trek up the Kelso Dunes, one of the tallest dune systems in America. The dunes have the rare ability to make a low rumbling sound when sand slides down the steep slopes. Some hikers liken these vibrations to singing or to a Tibetan gong.

Kelbaker Road, extending from Baker to Kelso, from I-15 to I-40, is the preserve's main route of travel and offers access to excellent hikes. Explore lava fields and cinder cones and hike to—and crawl through—narrow lava tubes.

A stop at the main Mojave National Preserve visitor center at the restored Kelso Depot is a must. Get oriented to the vast preserve, learn about its long, long roads and let the helpful staff assist with your itinerary. You want to make the most of your time—experiencing the preserve's considerable natural and historical treasures—not driving forever and ever.

The Preserve's maintained hiking trails are accessible by paved roads or well-graded dirt ones suitable for most passenger cars. In addition to its developed trails, the Preserve also has what it terms hiking "routes"—old Jeep roads or treks up washes, for example. Access to the trailheads for some routes requires a high-clearance vehicle; sometimes, due to weather or deteriorated road conditions, four-wheel drive is recommended. It's always a good idea to check on road conditions before driving to more remote trailheads.

No hiking trip would be complete without a descent into Hole-in-the-Wall via Rings Loop Trail.

Hole-in-the-Wall and Mid Hills are center-pieces of Mojave National Preserve. Both locales offer diverse desert scenery, fine campgrounds, and the feeling of being in the middle of nowhere though, in fact, located right in the middle of the preserve.

Hole-in-the-Wall is the kind of place Butch Cassidy and the Sundance Kid would choose as a hideout. Iron rings aid descent into Hole-in-the-Wall; this is definitely a hike to remember!

Kelso Dunes, the historic Kelso Depot, Hole-in-the-Wall and Mid Hills—the heart of the preserve can be viewed in a weekend. But there's so much more.

Meander through a "botanical island," the pinyon pine and juniper woodland in Caruthers Canyon. Or take a hike up Cima Dome, called the most symmetrical natural dome in the U.S.

On and around Cima Dome is the world's largest and densest Joshua tree forest. Botanists say the preserve's Joshuas are more symmetrical than their cousins elsewhere in the Mojave, though to me every tree looks different, each a rugged individualist.

To experience a really remote part of the preserve, hike to the ruins of Fort Piute. Wonder about the lonely life of the soldiers stationed there, marvel at the ruts carved into rock by the wheels of pioneer wagon trains; guess at the meaning of ancient petroglyphs.

Introduction

Finally, don't miss some great sights and great hikes just outside the preserve. If you're motoring to MNP on I-15, stop for a hike in intriguing Afton Canyon, a truly grand canyon of the Mojave River. Detour onto old Route 66 and take a hike over Hawaiian-like lava fields to Amboy Crater.

Hike smart, reconnect with nature and have a wonderful time on the trail.

Hike on.

—John McKinney

Mojave National Preserve

Geography

Mojave National Preserve totals some 1.6 million acres with 700,000 acres managed as wilderness. The Preserve is the third largest National Park Service holding outside of Alaska, behind only #1 Death Valley and #2 Yellowstone.

The Preserve is bounded north and south by I-15 and I-40, and on the east by U.S. Highway 95. The

The jagged, red-colored, spire-like Castle Peaks rise steeply from the surrounding New York Mountains.

area bounded by these three highways is dubbed "The Lonesome Triangle."

Elevation ranges from 880 feet at some flat spots near Baker to 7,929 feet atop Clark Mountain. The preserve is primarily a desert of mountains situated along north-south trending faults. Especially prominent is the southwest-northeast trending chain formed by the Granite, Providence, Mid Hill and New York ranges.

Natural History

"Mojave National Preserve is perhaps the last, large, natural, ecosystem-based national park unit likely to be created," stated Dennis Schramm, former Superintendent of Mojave National Preserve.

The desert tortoise, MNP's iconic but seldom-seen creature.

The preserve is a vast, mountainous land that represents a meeting of three great deserts—the Great Basin, Sonoran and Mojave. This meeting and mixing of ecosystems produces a wide variety of flora in combinations that exist nowhere else in the world.

Every feature visitors associate with the desert (sand dunes, grand mesas, dry lake beds, mountain ranges and more) is present in MNP, along with features not typically associated with a desert: limestone caves, lava flows and cinder cones.

The flora includes substantial Joshua tree woodland and lots of low desert scrub, of which the creosote bush is the most recognizable plant in this community; other plant life in the ecosystem includes brittlebush, ocotillo, burrobush, Bigelow's cholla, silver cholla, teddy bear and buckhorn cholla.

While hundreds of animals inhabit the preserve, visitors are likely to see only a few: jackrabbits, ravens and lizards. More easily observed bird species include the roadrunner, Costa's hummingbird, common raven and cactus wren.

Coreopsis, encelia, desert primrose, desert verbena and the blooms of the Mohave mound cactus are just a few of the more common Mojave wildflowers. Kelso Dunes and Ivanpah Valley are noted for their spring wildflower displays when conditions are right.

History

Ancient peoples are believed to have lived here up to 11,000 years ago. Prehistoric villages with rock shelters, petroglyphs and quarries have been found in the Providence Mountains; rock shelters and pictographs in the Granite Mountains; petroglyphs in the Cinder Cones and Lanfair Valley. Native people—Piutes, Mojave and Chemehuevi—were well-adapted to their environment and flourished until decimated and displaced in the mid-19th century.

Silver was first discovered in the 1860s. Mining put this part of the Mojave on the map. Gold, silver, zinc, iron ore and copper are among the array of

California Senator Alan Cranston worked tirelessly to protect the eastern Mojave Desert.

metallic elements that have been successfully mined. During the early 1900s, gold was discovered in the Castle Mountains, copper on Clark Mountain, zinc and silver at Mid Hills. During the 1940s, Kaiser Steel Company established the Vulcan Iron Ore Mine in the Providence Mountains. The successful mine created a short-lived boom in the town of Kelso, where most miners lived with their families.

Beginning in 1980, this portion of the Mojave was managed as East Mojave National Scenic Area by the U.S. Bureau of Land Management. For more than a decade, competing interests—miners, ranchers, off-road enthusiasts, scientists and conservationists—argued about what activities should be permitted in this desert.

In the landmark California Desert Protection Act of 1994, the eastern Mojave was transferred from BLM to National Park Service administration. Just before the bill's passage, anti-park legislators succeeded in altering Mojave's status from park to preserve, thus retaining certain forms of hunting, grazing and mining.

Administration

Mojave National Preserve (http://www.nps.gov/moja) is administered by the National Park Service. The restored Kelso Depot is now the primary visitor center for the preserve. Kelso Depot Visitor Center

(760-252-6108) offers information, interpretive exhibits, an art gallery, bookstore, water, restrooms and a picnic area. (Hours can vary, subject to closure.) From I-15 in Baker, exit on Kelbaker Road and drive 35 miles southeast to Kelso.

Hole-in-the-Wall Information Center (760-252-6104 or 760-928-2572) features information, a bookstore, campgrounds, picnic area, water and restrooms. From October through April it's open Wednesday through Sunday from 9 a.m. to 4 p.m., and from May through September, Saturdays only, from 10 a.m. to 4 p.m. (Hours can vary, subject to closure.)

Headquarters (Barstow) Information Center (760-252-6100) has exhibits, bookstore and restrooms. It's open Monday through Friday, 8 a.m. to 4:30 p.m. From I-15 in Barstow, exit on Barstow Road and drive south to 2701 Barstow Road.

Rails and trails in stunning Afton Canyon.

EVERY TRAIL TELLS A STORY.

I
OFF I-15

HIKE ON.

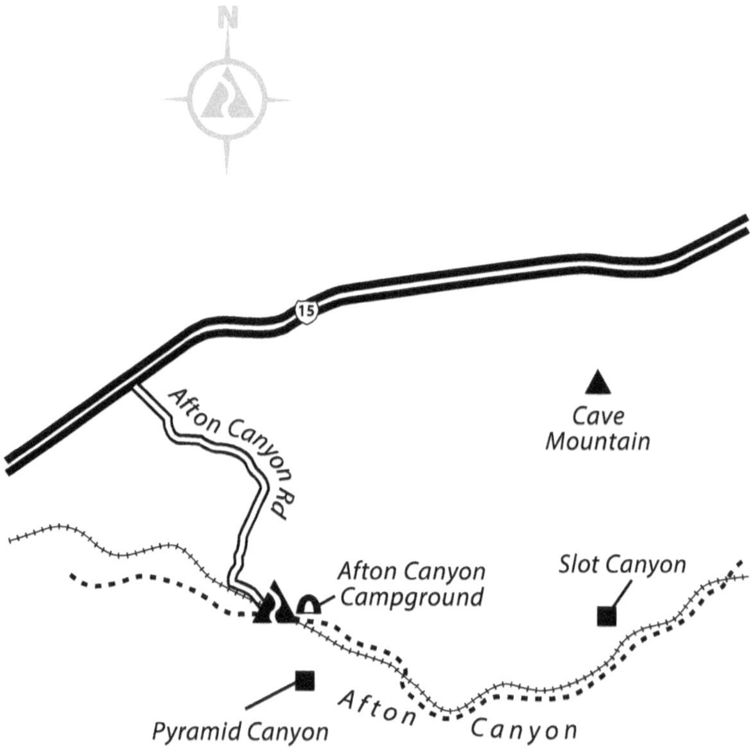

Afton Canyon

Afton Canyon Trail

6.5 miles round trip or longer

A long and deep gorge with sheer walls that rise 600 feet above the canyon floor, Afton Canyon has been referred to as the "Grand Canyon of the Mojave." The narrowest parts of the canyon offer some intriguing hikes.

Afton Canyon Natural Area, 42,000 acres under the administration of the U.S. Bureau of Land Management, borders Mojave National Preserve on the northwest, and is one of the most conveniently located sites in the eastern Mojave. If you see a great many 4x4s zooming around or visitors collecting rocks and minerals, remember this is BLM land, not national parkland, and such activities are permitted.

Afton Canyon is one of the few places where the Mojave River runs year-round. This dependable source of water supports a variety of plants including cottonwoods, willows, rabbit bush, smoke trees and grasses.

Native and migratory birds are attracted to the site, including herons, egrets, killdeer and ibis. California mud turtles, frogs, minnows and the Mohave chub live in the river or along the shore.

The canyon has benefited from more than three decades of environmental restoration efforts. The Mojave Road in Afton Canyon was re-routed in order to protect sensitive riparian environment, and off-highway vehicles are now prohibited in the area. Botanists and hard-working volunteers have waged war against the invasive tamarisk, which chokes out native species. Ridding the canyon of tamarisk allows a more oasis-like streamside community to thrive.

Ah, the sight and sound of a mighty locomotive powering across gleaming trestles!

Rail fans will delight in the number of freight trains that regularly pass through the canyon.

The 8-mile-length of Afton Canyon is an intriguing out-and-back hike; however, most hikers prefer sampling the canyon with a more modest 5- to 6-mile jaunt. The short walk along the riverbed from the campground to the railroad trestle is a favorite family-friendly exploration. You may also explore side canyons, such as Pyramid Canyon.

DIRECTIONS: Take the Afton exit off Interstate 15, 33 miles east of Barstow; the graded

3-mile-long road leads to the campground in Afton Canyon. Park at the campground.

THE HIKE: As you hike the canyon, look for an old mine on the south wall. Although it appears to be an abandoned gold mine, it never produced as promised. Years ago, the unscrupulous owner of the mine simply salted it with gold in order to sell worthless shares to unwitting investors.

Continuing east, notice a number of side canyons situated on the north wall of Afton Canyon. These side canyons are most obvious when you look for the man-made culverts that have been placed to prevent further water erosion.

At the culvert marked 192.99, observe another canyon that features magnificently eroded shapes. At the culvert marked 194.65, take a flashlight to explore a fascinating cave/canyon that twists and turns.

Beyond this point the canyon widens and holds less interest for the hiker. Afton Canyon extends a few more miles to a double trestle bridge near Cave Mountain. For a different perspective of the canyon, consider returning via the river bottom.

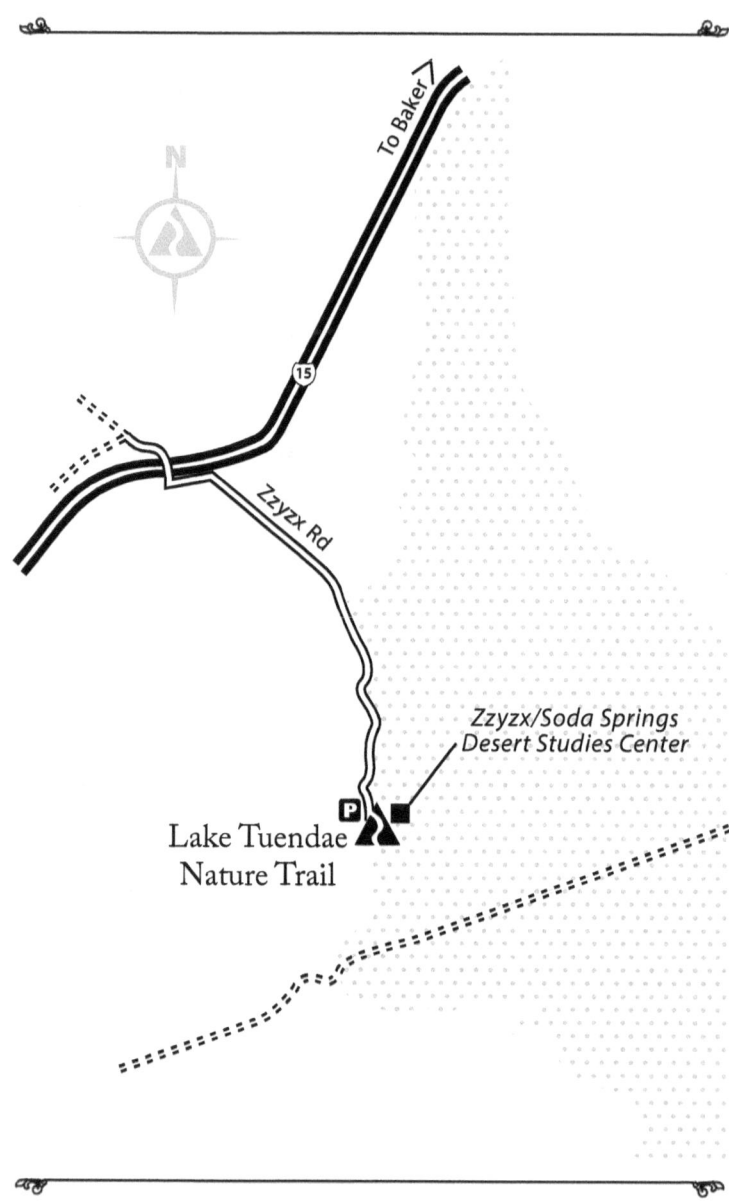

Zzyzx & Soda Springs
Lake Tuendae Nature Trail

0.25-mile loop

One of the most fascinating places in MNP, Soda Springs has a unique ecology and a long and colorful history. Get off I-15, take a short hike, and learn about the the story behind Zzyzx.

Native people lived here during the Pleistocene Period (8,000 bc) and their descendants left archeological evidence of continued occupation through the mid-1800s. From 1860 to 1868, the U.S. Army maintained an outpost at Soda Springs. Thereafter the outpost became a commercial rest stop.

From 1944 through 1974, thanks to the efforts of Dr. Curtis Springer, Soda Springs turned into Zzyzx Mineral Springs and Health Resort that promised health to its thousands of visitors and financial supporters.

A labor force recruited from L.A.'s Skid Row built the resort's extensive facilities. A 60-room hotel called The Castle, a dining hall, indoor baths and a large swimming pool shaped in the form of a cross were among the original projects. Springer broadcast his daily religious programs from his powerful radio station, and conducted services at the Zzyzx Community Church. With no utility services, the entire development was self-contained and energy-efficient.

The main road in the complex was named "Boulevard of Dreams," and for many years it was a fitting title. For 30 years, believers, health-seekers and the curious flocked to Zzyzx, lured by Springer's promises, products, "Hot Mineral Water baths, matchless climate and wonderful foods." Although he never attached a fee to his concoctions or services, the donations poured in; Springer's annual income was estimated at between $250,000 and $750,000.

U.S. authorities cracked down hard on "Doc Springer," as he was known to his detractors. He was charged with income tax evasion by the Internal Revenue Service; called "King of the Quacks" by the American Medical Association; convicted of false advertising by the Pure Food and Drug Administration and his land and Zzyzx facilities were confiscated by the Bureau of Land Management. Springer never returned to the resort after he was evicted in 1974, and he died in 1985.

Soda Springs today hosts The Desert Studies Center, a field station of the California State University system. Nearby is a diversity of environments:

creosote scrub, springs, sand dunes, mesquite thickets, rocky slopes and ravines.

The minnow-sized Mojave Tui chub survives in shallow ponds along with another Mojave native, the Saratoga Spring pupfish. Birdwatchers have recorded sightings of more than 200 species in MNP.

DIRECTIONS: From Interstate 15, about 6 miles southwest of Baker and 60 miles northeast of Barstow, exit on Zzyzx Road and travel 4.5 miles south to the parking area and trailhead.

THE HIKE: Exhibits along the interpretive trail reveal the rich natural and cultural history of this curious place. Walk the grounds of Zzyzx (where permitted). Some of Springer's buildings are still in use, although many have been rebuilt or improved.

"Lake" Tuendae, a curious reminder of huckster-evangelist Doc Springer's so-called health resort.

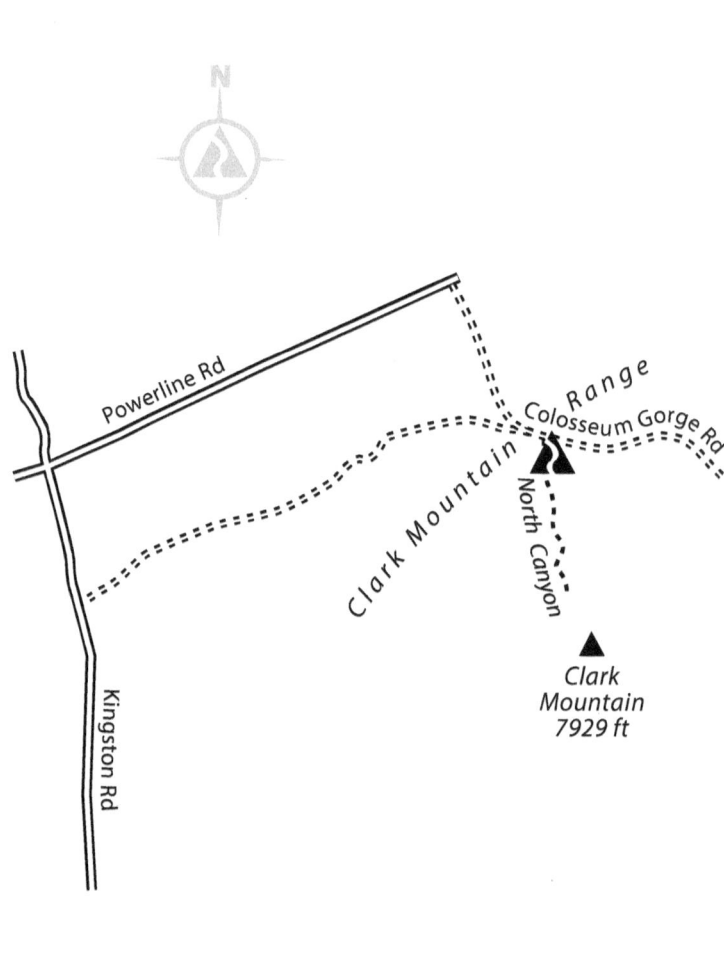

CLARK MOUNTAIN
NORTH CANYON TRAIL

To summit is 5 miles round trip

At 7,929 feet, Clark Mountain is the tallest peak in Mojave National Preserve. Because the peak is a bit geographically isolated from the main part of the Clark Mountain Range situated to the northeast, it's a distinct landmark, easy to recognize even when viewed from many miles away. Clark Mountain is also isolated from the main part of the preserve—the only section located north of Interstate 15.

You can sample the scenery of the rugged mountain, dotted with the Mojave's largest stand of white fir, with a short hike up Fir Canyon—sometimes called North Canyon. But be prepared: Clark Mountain is in a very remote part of MNP and 4WD is highly recommended to access it.

Native people, including the Chemehuevi, Piute and Mohave inhabited the Clark Mountains for thousands of years. Archeologists have discovered petroglyphs, rock shelters and rock alignments, plus large ash-filled pits where native people once roasted agave for food. Experts suggest that native people may have considered the mountain a spiritually significant site.

Clark Mountain was mined for more than a century and significant amounts of silver, gold, copper and several other rare, precious and semi-precious materials including turquoise. Nowadays the bulk of Clark Mountain is wilderness and most mining is concentrated at the southern base of the mountain—long-established rare-earth mines operated by the Molybdenum Corporation of America.

The mountain is the subject of one of the Mojave's most colorful mining tales: The Lost River of Gold. A 1920s miner, Earl Dorr, tried to convince investors to finance his discovery in Crystal Cave—a 3,000-foot deep river through the mountains, its sands filled with gold. Dorr gained financial backing and struck a rich vein, all right, but it was zinc, not gold. The Lost River of Gold was never found but the legend lives on.

Clark Mountain supports a number of plant communities, offering habitat for several animal species. A sizeable population of bighorn sheep thrives here, as do raptors, feral burros, and several varieties of snakes and lizards.

DIRECTIONS: From I-15, 25 miles northeast of Baker, exit on Excelsior Mine Road and travel 7.7 miles on paved road to "Powerline Road" (a graded road that leads along a powerline corridor. Turn right (east) and travel 5.7 miles on rougher road to the first junction with an unsigned southbound road. Head south on this road toward Clark Mountain and into Mojave National Preserve. About 2.5 miles from the Powerline Road, pass a junction with a 4WD road on the right and continue with the main road, bending east for another 0.5 mile. Look for a steel-post closed-off old road on the right (south) with a wilderness boundary sign and park nearby at a wide spot in the road.

THE HIKE: Ascend the old jeep road into a pinyon pine and juniper woodland. Look up at the striking cliffs on Clark's crest. At 1.5 miles, the canyon narrows, closed-in by high volcanic walls.

Two miles out, you reach the end of the road and an impossible to surmount dry fall—nature's way of telling you to turnaround.

Get great views of the Granite Mountains from Kelbaker Road, MNP's "Main Street."

EVERY TRAIL TELLS A STORY.

II
Kelbaker Road & Heart of the Preserve

HIKE ON.

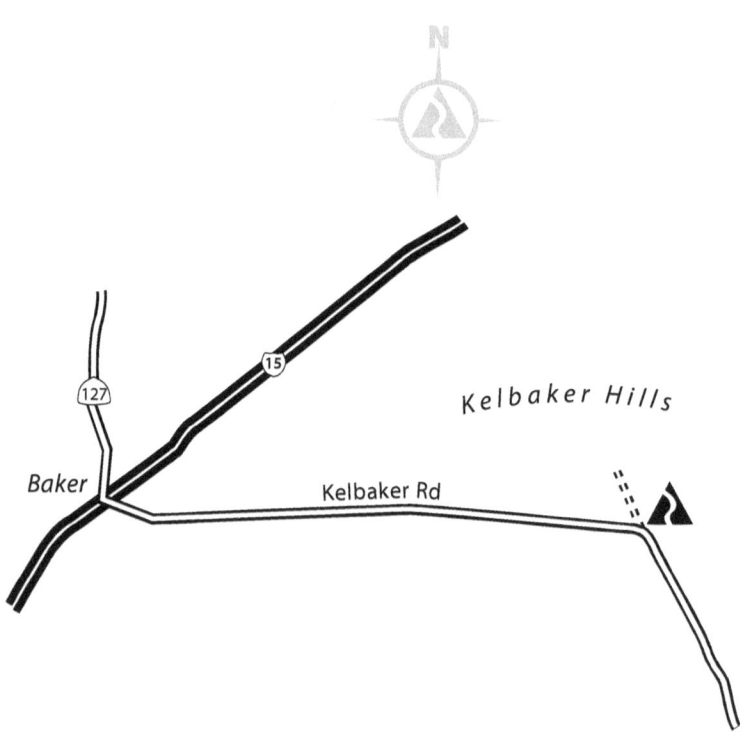

Kelbaker Hills

Kelbaker Hills Trail

2 miles round trip with 300-foot elevation gain

Preserve visitors who remain in their vehicles when driving Kelbaker Road from Baker to the Kelso Depot Visitor Center miss intriguing sites en route. Two favorites along the way are the Kelbaker Hills and Lava Beds (see hike description).

If Mojave National Preserve had a Main Street, Kelbaker Road would be it. The road is the Preserve's busiest, and provides access to several of the most popular attractions.

But it wasn't always a breeze to zoom across the desert from I-15 to I-40. "At Kelso, we took on supplies and found that Baker lay just across another small range…" wrote Edna Calkins Price in *Burro Bill and Me*, an account of her travels in the Mojave in the 1930s. "Thirty six miles away, just twelve hours of merciless walking."

In 1999, the National Park Service installed a large Mojave National Preserve entry sign just outside of Baker on Kelbaker Road. The entry monument, one of those grand granite proclamations characteristic of other national parks, emphasizes Kelbaker's status as the major Mojave road.

Here's your chance to name one of the preserve's geographic features. I call them the Kelbaker Hills because of their proximity to Kelbaker Road as well as for their location a dozen miles southeast of Baker and two-dozen miles northwest of Kelso; however, they don't really have a name on the map or one in common usage. Others have suggested the "Baker Hills" due to their close-to-town position or the "Rhyolite Hills" because of their volcanic composition.

By whatever name, these hills offer a close-to-the-paved road wilderness experience, as well as a short (though moderately strenuous) hike.

DIRECTIONS: From Interstate 15 in Baker, drive 11 miles east on Kelbaker Road. Just as the road makes a pronounced bend right (south) turn left (north) on the unsigned dirt road. Drive 0.8 mile along the preserve's signed wilderness boundary. Look east of the road for a distinct gap in the Kelbaker Hills and scarce parking just east off the road where you can find it.

THE HIKE: If you locate a sketchy old road extending east up the wash leading to the hills, take it;

otherwise, simply walk up the wash toward the obvious gap in the hills. Your route will angle toward the base of the tallest hills, and just to the left of them.

A bit more than 0.5 mile out, observe a couple of narrow ravines (favorite burro routes, judging by the tracks) that lead to the top of the hills. Climb (careful, it's loose footing) any one of these ravines for good views of this part of the Preserve.

Experienced rock-scramblers can make their way to the top of the highest hills. Those determined to make a loop hike out of this jaunt can do so by descending a ravine southeasterly and junctioning the main wash that leads back to the gap in the hills, and then returning to the trailhead.

Out-of-the-way sights in out-of-the-way places: a jack-o'-lantern in the Kelbaker Hills!

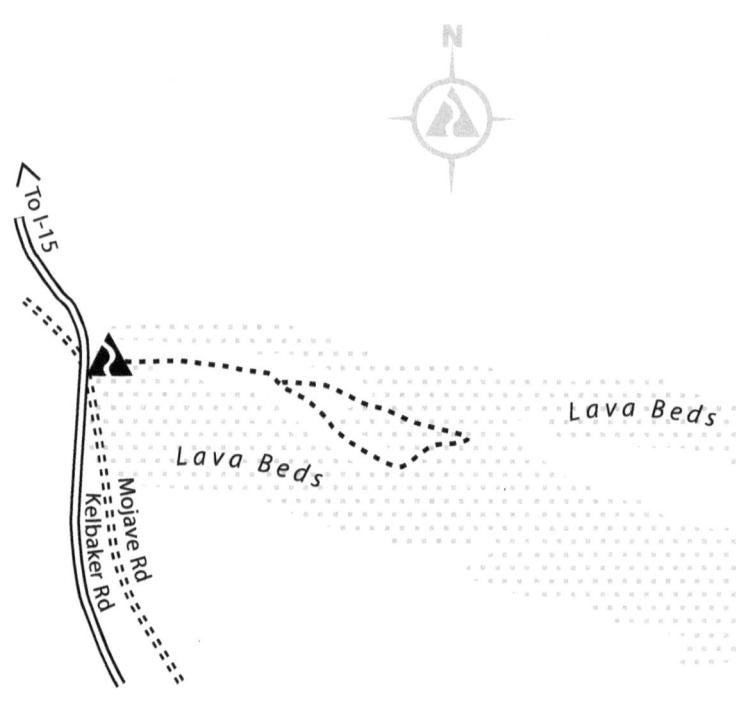

Lava Beds

Lava Beds Trail

1.2-mile loop

Kelbaker Road is more than a beeline from Baker to Kelso, from I-15 to I-40. It also gives access to the vast Lava-Land in the northwest part of Mojave National Preserve.

One particularly intriguing sight-to-see from the road is the line of Cinder Cones, 32 mounds of red and black rocks, rising as if from nowhere above the desert landscape. These little volcanoes began erupting some 7.6 million years ago but don't call them "ancient"! Lava last flowed just 10,000 years ago.

All lava is not created equally and lava flows in different ways depending on its consistency. Some lava is thick and gooey and doesn't flow very far very fast. Geologists say lava in MNP is a runny balsaltic sort and flows like maple syrup. It cooled at various rates, creating the tunnels, tubes and formations we see today.

The preserve's northern lava beds can be explored by a short hike off Kelbaker Road.

A wash extending alongside the lava formation gives the hiker a convenient thoroughfare as well as a close-up view of the volcanic cliff face.

This look at the lava resembles those hillside cuts made by highway-makers, though it was nature, not a road crew that, revealed the lava beds. Green, gray and red lichen color the north side of the lava outcroppings.

BTW there's more to this hike than igneous rock. The lava landscape is dotted with beavertail, barrel and cholla cactus, as well as yucca and creosote. And there are some petroglyphs etched on the dark rock.

DIRECTIONS: From Baker and I-15, head 14.2 miles south on Kelbaker Road to the Lava Beds and an unsigned turnout on your left. The turnout is just south of the long, narrow beds and just north of a wash. (Hint: if Kelbaker Road takes you through a major gap in the Lava Beds, you ventured about 0.4 mile too far south of the trailhead for this little exploration.)

THE HIKE: From the trailhead, ascend to the protrusion of lava a bit above and to the right. Head east on a faint, but visible trail at the base of the lava beds. Look for a bend in the historic Mojave Road. Marvel at the odd geology as you walk 0.6 mile to trail's end.

Scramble to the top of the lava beds and a miniature plateau paved with a mosaic of lava talus that resembles the ruins of an ancient Roman Empire road.

You can extend your Lava Beds exploration a mile with a bit of cross-country hiking. Continue another (trail-less) half mile east along a ridge, then descend north into a wash. The wash can be followed west to connect back with the trail and trailhead.

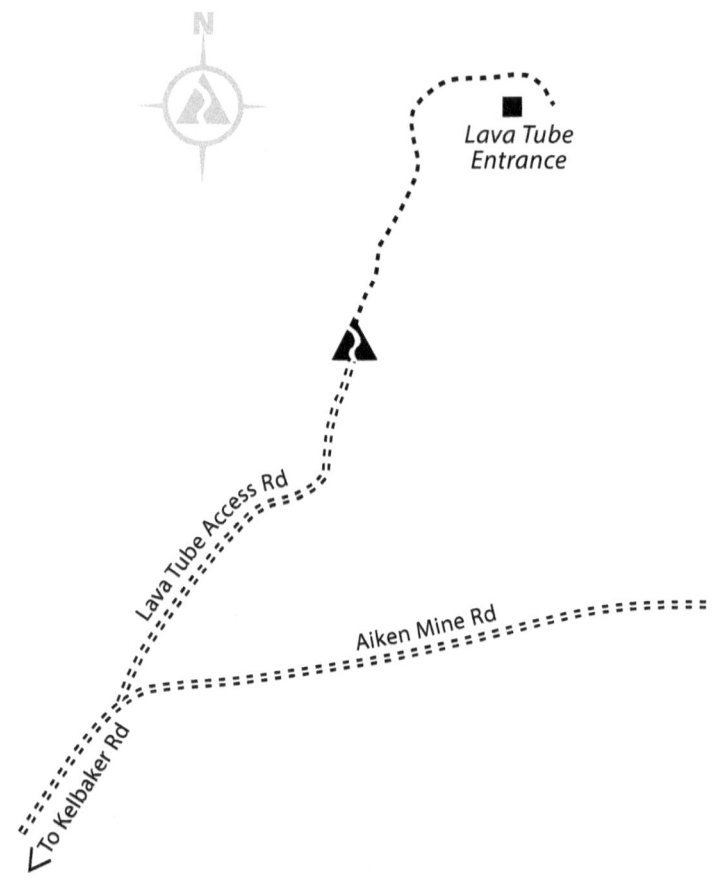

Lava Tube & Cinder Cones

To Lava Tube is 0.5 mile round trip; to Cinder Cone is 1.5 mile round trip

Explore a lava tube and climb a cinder cone on this short, interesting hike through an almost eerie red-black moonscape.

During a long-ago volcanic eruption when swift-moving lava flowed over the land, the lava tube was formed when the inner flow cooled more quickly than the outer flow. Today, the resulting cave-like formation appears to be a great hole in the earth.

A ladder in the tube facilitates climbing down into it; use caution as you maneuver into the tube. Making your way through the underground tube requires some bending and stretching. Bring a flashlight or headlamp to explore the cave's nooks and crannies.

After your underground tour, explore the 25,600-acre area designated Cinder Cone National Natural Landmark in 1973. Consisting of 32 volcanic formations, the cones are thought to date back 10 million years.

Legend has it that the Apollo astronauts trained on this moon-like surface in preparation for their historic 1969 lunar landing. But officials deny that such maneuvers ever occurred. Nevertheless, you can easily imagine the space-suited explorers bounding around the Cinder Cones.

Neil Armstrong may not have taken even one small step for man on this volcanic field, but it does attract geologists from all over the world. The composition of the rock is said to be denser than anywhere on earth; it provides scientists with important information about geologic processes below the earth's surface.

For more than 20 years the Aiken Mine (closed in 1990) hauled away one of the cinder cones by the ton. The lightweight reddish material ended up lining gardens and walkways of suburban homes and offices. The mine site is a blight on the land, but is an intriguing place to visit for the opportunity to peer into the inside of a cinder cone. (From the turnoff to the trailhead, continue north on Aiken Mine Road another 2.5 miles.)

DIRECTIONS: From Interstate 15 in Baker, head south on Kelbaker Road to Aikens Mine Road. Turn left (north) on the unpaved road (high-clearance vehicles suggested and in adverse conditions four-wheel drive may be required) and drive 4.3 miles to a fork in the road and bear left. Continue

0.25 mile to the signed trailhead and large circular parking area.

THE HIKE: Hike north uphill on a very rough old road for about 0.2 mile. Look right for a narrow trail (sometimes signed with a rock cairn or metal post) and follow it to the entrance of the lava tube.

Descend the narrow steel ladder to the floor of the main cavern. The cool, dark underground area is a welcome retreat from often-scorching outdoor temperatures and unrelenting sunlight; you might spot bats or owls that inhabit the cave. Enjoy the unique setting, especially the beams of light that flood sections of the tube.

Back above ground, hike north to the closest cinder cone. Climb to the top for a great view of the other cones and the vast landscape beyond.

Touched by the light in the mysterious Lava Tube.

The restored Kelso Depot now serves as the Mojave National Preserve Visitor Center.

Kelso Depot Visitor Center

Depot Walkabout

0.25 mile stroll

After five years of restoration efforts, Kelso Depot Information Center opened in 2005 and gave the preserve a long-needed visitor focal point similar to that in other national parklands. The historic depot, which once served as a train station, lunch room and employee dormitory has been transformed into MNP's chief information center. It's a delight to walk through this place, closed for so long, and now so accessible.

Exhibits highlight the history and natural history of the surrounding desert: mining, ranching, sand dunes and the desert tortoise. Period furnishings in the old baggage room, ticket office and other rooms evoke the feel of railroad travel in the early decades of the 20th century. The center also boasts a theater, bookstore, restrooms, a picnic area, and an old-fashioned lunch counter.

In 1906, the completion of the railroad between Salt Lake City and the port facilities in Los Angeles led to the development of the tiny town of Kelso located, as the railroad described it, "235 track miles from Los Angeles." Because Kelso was one of the few places in the desert with access to dependable water sources, it was considered a good location for a railroad stopping point.

The Spanish Revival-style depot, designed with a red-tiled roof, graceful arches, and a red brick platform was built in 1924. It featured accommodations for railroad employees, a billiard room, library, a telegraph office, and a waiting room for passengers. Nicknamed "The Beanery," the restaurant served meals to passengers traveling on trains without dining cars.

When Union Pacific officials decided to demolish the historic structure in 1985, local citizens, governmental officials, environmentalists and a host of others formed a coalition to fight the plan. The group, known as the Kelso Depot Fund, was successful in its efforts to save the depot.

DIRECTIONS: Kelso Depot Visitor Center is located at the intersection of Kelbaker Road and Kelso-Cima Road (Mojave's two primary trans-preserve roads). From I-15 in Baker, exit on Kelbaker Road and travel 35 miles southeast to Kelso. From I-40, exit on Kelbaker Road and drive 22 miles north. (760-252-6108)

THE HIKE: On your walk around what is often called a ghost town, take in the old jail and post office, which was built in the 1930s and also served as a grocery store. The few abandoned houses and foundation ruins hardly seem to suggest that during World War II years the population of Kelso increased to nearly 2,000 residents—primarily railroad employees and workers at the Vulcan Iron Ore Mine located in the nearby Providence Mountains. The railroad was used extensively to haul the mined ore to its milling site in Fontana. But when the mine shut down in 1947, the town's population dwindled.

Date palms and cottonwoods add to an oasis-like feeling. Although they no longer stop here, freight trains regularly rumble through Kelso, adding a nostalgic touch to this picturesque setting.

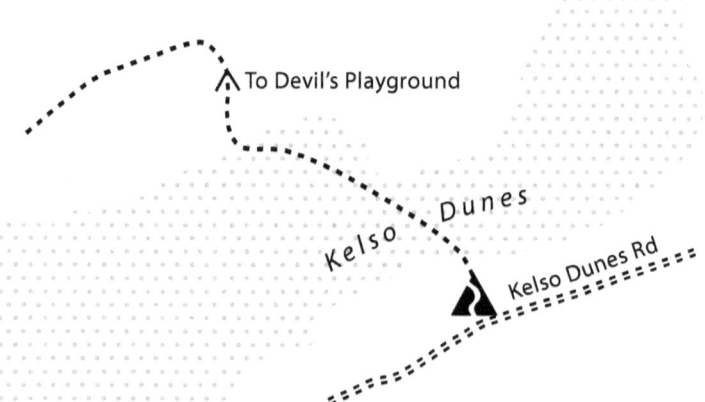

Kelso Dunes

Kelso Dunes Trail

To top of Kelso Dunes is 3 miles roundtrip with 400-foot elevation gain

Kelso Dunes, one of the tallest dune systems in America, is a must-see sight for any MNP visitor and a great hike. The dunes are known to give off good vibrations.

The Kelso Dunes have the rare ability to make a low rumbling sound when sand slides down the steep slopes. This sound has been variously described as that of a kettle drum, low flying airplane, singing or Tibetan gong.

The sand that forms Kelso Dunes blows in from the Mojave River basin. After traveling east 35 miles across a stark plain known as the Devil's Playground, it's deposited in hills nearly 600 feet high. Westerlies carrying the sand rush headlong into winds from other directions, which is why the sand is dropped here, and why it stays here.

For further confirmation of the circular pattern of winds that formed the dunes, examine the bunches of grass on the lower slopes. Notice that the tips of the tall grasses have etched 360-degree circles on the sand.

Other patterns on the sand are made by the desert's abundant, but rarely seen, wildlife. Look for the tracks of a coyote, kit fox, antelope ground squirrel, packrat, raven, sidewinder, lizards and mice.

DIRECTIONS: From Interstate 15 in Baker, some 60 miles northeast of Barstow, turn south on Kelbaker Road and proceed about 35 miles to the Kelso Depot Visitor Center. Continue on Kelbaker Road for another 7 miles to a signed dirt road and turn west (right). Drive 3 miles to a parking area. The trail begins just beyond some NPS interpretive displays.

THE HIKE: Stick with the footpath and its northwesterly course as long as it lasts. Once the trail peters out, angle toward the low saddle atop the dunes, just to the right of the highest point.

(Know the old saying "One step forward, two steps back"? This saying will take on new meaning if you attempt to take the most direct route to the top of the dunes by hiking straight up the tallest sand hill.)

Cross the lower dunes, dotted with mesquite and creosote bushes, and in spring bedecked with yellow and white desert primrose, pink sand verbena and yellow sunflowers.

Kelso Dunes

At the saddle located to the right of the high point, turn left and trek another hundred yards or so to the top. The black material crowning the top of the dunes is magnetite, an iron oxide.

The view from the top takes in the vast dunes complex, the Kelso Mountains to the north, the Bristol Mountains to the southwest, the Granite Mountains to the south, the Providence Mountains to the east.

While atop the dunes, perhaps your footsteps will cause mini-avalanches and the dunes will sha-boom-sha-boom for you. The extreme dryness of this locale, combined with the wind-polished, rounded nature of the individual sand grains, may have something to do with the dunes' musical ability. After enjoying the sights and sounds, descend the steep dune face (much easier on the way down!) and return to the trailhead.

Kelso Dunes, one of the tallest dune systems in America and top of the MNP's "Must Hike" list.

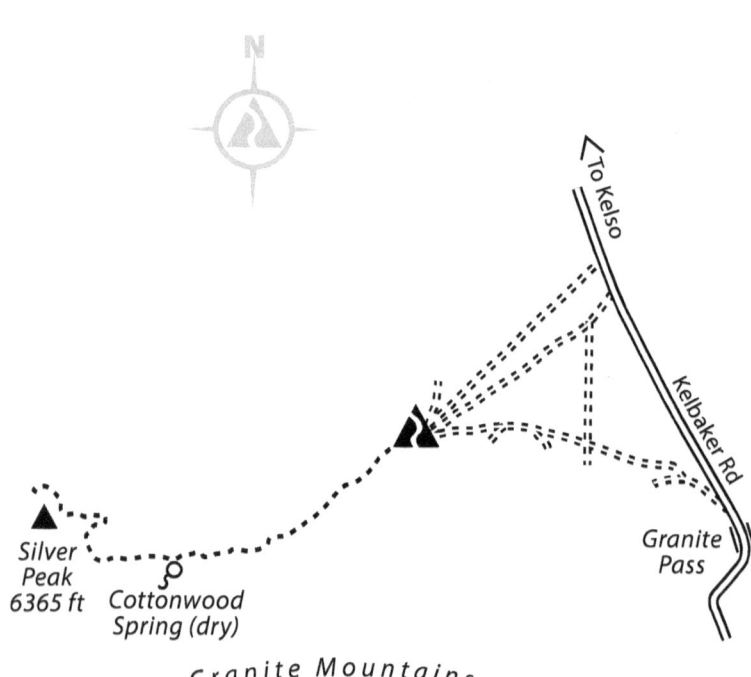

GRANITE MOUNTAINS
SILVER PEAK TRAIL

To Silver Peak is 8.6 miles round trip with 2,400 foot elevation gain

A little-visited wilderness, the Granite Mountains are southernmost in a chain of mountains that trends southwest-northeast across MNP. The craggy shoulders of these 6,000-foot mountains are the domain of desert bighorn sheep.

Silver Peak (6,365 feet) is not the highest summit in the rugged and highly eroded Granite Mountains (that honor belongs to Granite Mountain, the 6,762-foot signature summit located a few miles south of Silver Peak), but it does boast the only reasonably hike-able trail in the range. Reward for the steep climb to Silver Peak are grand vistas of Cima Dome, the Providence Mountains and Kelso Dunes.

In addition to being part of MNP, a portion of these mountains are part of the University of California's Natural Reserve System. Avoid disturbing any of the natural sciences projects conducted by the Granite Mountains Desert Research Center by staying on the area's main trails. Researchers have tallied more than 460 species of plants, 34 species of reptiles and 130 species of birds.

The rapid change in elevation along Silver Peak Trail is accompanied by distinct changes in vegetation. At lower elevations in Cottonwood Wash, sage and yucca are among the dominant plants. Higher elevations bring cholla-dotted slopes and then a woodland of pinyon pine and juniper.

DIRECTIONS: From Interstate 40 drive 10 miles north on Kelbaker Road. Look left (west) for an unsigned dirt road. (Clue: another dirt road, nearly opposite this one, heads east from the other side of Kelbaker Road.) Those traveling from northern preserve locations on Kelbaker Road will find the above-mentioned turnoff about 4.6 miles south of the turnoff for Kelso Dunes. Drive 1.75 miles on the narrow dirt road to a small rise, where there is a primitive camping area and the signed boundary of the wilderness.

THE HIKE: From the trailhead, gaze up at your destination, Silver Peak, and head west into Cottonwood Wash. Reminders of the area's ranching days come in the form of fencing and dirt tracks leading off to water tanks and corrals. After 0.2 mile, the trail/wash route forks. Stay right, join the jeep road, sticking with the dirt road (as opposed to the sandy wash) to the right of the corral.

Mainly it's a gradual ascent and a straight shot toward the base of Silver Peak.

After about 2.5 miles, the old road narrows and begins a more aggressive ascent up Silver Peak. The steep path (very steep—it gains 1500 feet in the next 2 miles) and as it climbs north passes amidst pinyon pine and juniper.

After turning south, the path suddenly ends about 0.2 mile and 300 feet in elevation short of the summit. With the help of cairns, pick your way over a very steep and rocky slope to the summit.

The curious and seldom visited Granite Mountains.

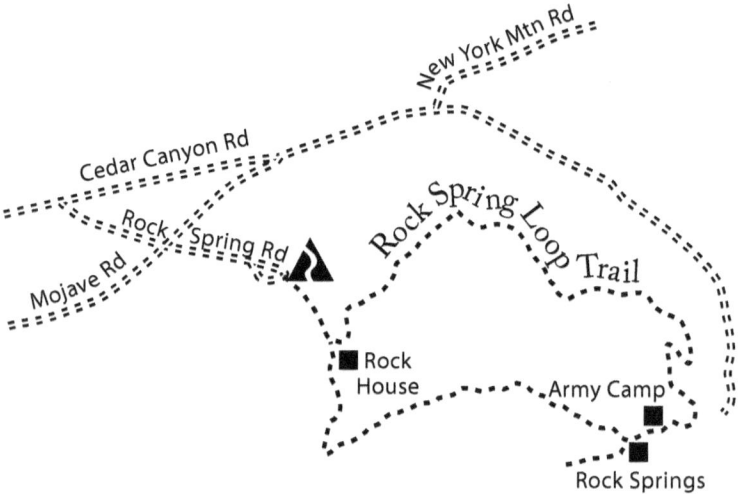

Rock Spring

Rock Spring Loop Trail

1.2-mile loop

Reliable watering holes in the Mojave are few and far between so it's not surprising to learn that Rock Spring has been a precious resource for Mojave and Chemehuevi Indians, ranchers, miners, the U.S. Army and generations of desert travelers. Discover the colorful story of Rock Spring from interpretive exhibits along an easy-to-hike loop trail.

Water there was and is (ranging from a trickle to deep pools) at Rock Spring but little else except solitude and stone. The considerable stone was put to good use in building the Rock House, still standing a short walk from the trailhead.

Told by doctors he didn't have long to live, World War I vet and poison-gas attack victim Bert Smith came to the Mojave to heal. Smith built the Rock House in 1929; apparently the climate agreed with him because he lived 25 more years. During the 1980s artist Carl Faber lived and worked at Rock House, selling his paintings to passersby.

In 1866, a U.S. Army report described Camp Rock Spring as "a forlorn military post consisting of one officer and perhaps a dozen men guarding the springs and road there." Set up to protect U.S. mail carriers along the Mojave Road, the post was abandoned after just 15 months.

The loop trail is more than a history lesson and has its botanical highlights as well. High desert flora flourishes here at an elevation of nearly 5,000 feet: Mojave sage, yucca, buckhorn cholla, cliff rose and juniper trees.

DIRECTIONS: From Hole-in-the-Wall Visitor Center, head west on Black Canyon Road to its intersection with Cedar Canyon Road. Turn right (east) and drive 5 miles to the signed turnoff for Rock Spring. Follow Rock Spring Road 0.25 mile to road's end and the trailhead.

THE HIKE: Walk to the Rock House and check out its sturdy construction, with walls nearly two feet thick. From the west end of the house, the signed path heads briefly south before bending east.

Look for the foundation ruins of a 1930s-era mill that crushed rock to release the copper within. The rock from nearby Watson Wash was not high quality and the enterprise was soon abandoned.

The path descends through a short narrow canyon to a stone perch above a wash and interpretive signage located near Rock Spring, where water is nearly always present. The spring attracts birds, wildlife and Famed Mojave Road linked this spring and others located about 20 to 30 miles apart—a natural, all be it challenging, travel route.

If you descend into the wash and head right (up-creek), you can spot petroglyphs etched onto the granite walls. (Don't climb on the rocks or touch the petroglyphs.) On the opposite wall, look for the name of a Camp Rock Spring soldier inscribed in the rock.

From Rock Spring, the trail ascends to a ridge for excellent vistas of the New York and Hackberry mountains, as well as the historic Mojave Road, now a four-wheel drive route. The path passes a cluster of pinyon pine and juniper before returning to Rock House and the trailhead.

The Rock House: A nice place to visit but you wouldn't want to live there.

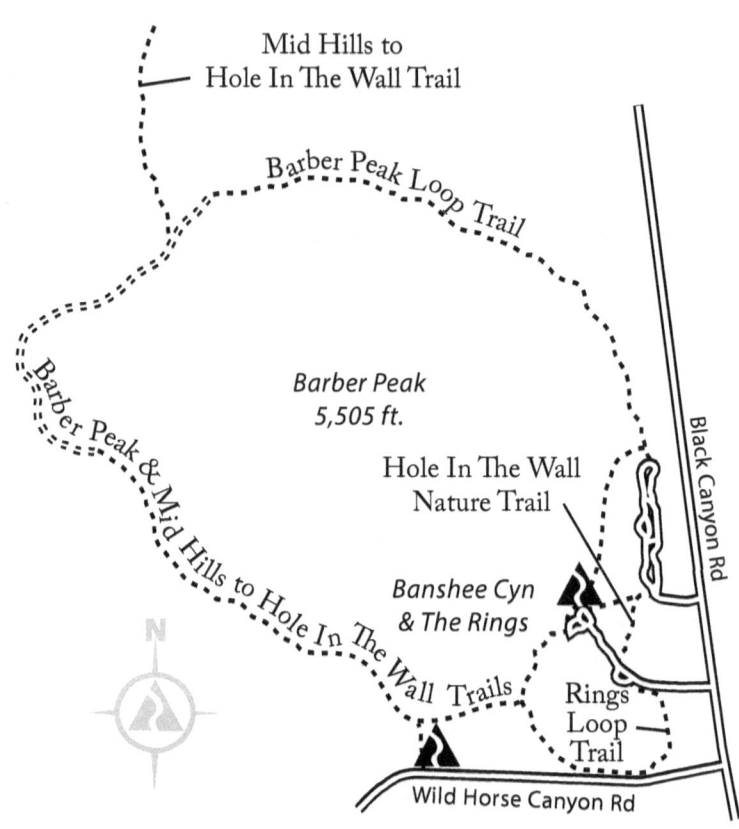

HOLE-IN-THE-WALL
Rings Loop Trail

1.5-mile loop

To Hole-in-the-Wall is 2 miles round trip

A fine camping area, outstanding views of the surrounding mountains, and an unforgettable hiking experience attract visitors to Hole-in-the-Wall.

Hikers once used ropes and ladders to descend into the maze of volcanic rocks from the campground area; today the descent is accomplished by negotiating two sets of iron rings that have been set into the rock. Maneuvering through the rings is not particularly difficult for those who are reasonably agile and take their time. But acrophobes or claustrophobes may want to pass on this adventure.

As the story goes, in the 1880s, a couple of ranch hands were searching for some stray cattle, and they came upon a pair of Indians who were leading a few cattle. Suspecting them of stealing their stock, the ranch hands chased the Indians into a canyon, which they thought was a dead-end. To their amazement, the Indians scrambled up the rocks in the lower canyon, and then disappeared—seemingly right into the blank wall. The men concluded the Indians must have found or created a hole in the wall.

Hole-in-the-Wall rocks have a violent past—geologically speaking, that is. Some 18 million years ago, a volcano in the Woods Mountains erupted and spewed ash and rocks (some 60 feet across—among the largest ever documented!). Hot ashes cremated every living thing in the area; countless plant and animal fossils lie entombed beneath the volcanic tuff of Hole-in-the-Wall's cliffs.

Look for faint petroglyphs on the rocks about 0.25 mile from the trailhead. (Don't touch the rock art or climb on the rocks.

DIRECTIONS: From Interstate 40, approximately 42 miles west of Needles and nearly 100 miles east of Barstow, exit on Essex Road. Head north 9.5 miles and bear right on Black Canyon Road, which soon turns to dirt. Continue 10 miles to Hole-in-the-Wall.

THE HIKE: The path plunges into a wall of rocks. Grasp the iron rings and lower yourself into Banshee Canyon. Descend amidst impressive pockmarked canyon walls. You can turn around at the canyon bottom or continue as your route curves north toward Wild Horse Canyon.

Banshee Canyon is named not for the shrieking elves of the Scottish Highlands, but for the sounds said to be heard here at night that resemble their cries. Horned owls and the sound of the wind whistling through the holes make a quiet night in the canyon unlikely.

Enjoy exploring the volcanic rock formations known as rhyolite, a crystallized form of lava. The holes provide frames for taking silly photographs. Look for any number of raptors circling overhead: golden eagles, hawks and owls.

Follow Banshee Canyon to its opening, then south out into the open desert. Pass a junction with Barber Peak Trail and continue on Rings Trail as it bends east then north to a second trailhead by the visitor information center and walk 0.25 up the dirt road to return to the starting trailhead.

Hole-in-the-Wall Visitor Center is located right in the middle of the stunning rock formations that comprise Hole-in-the-Wall.

TheTrailmaster.com

HOLE-IN-THE-WALL INFORMATION CENTER

Nature Trail

0.5 mile round trip

Hole-in-the-Wall Information Center offers a bookstore, picnic area and campground. Rangers give talks about the area's rock art and unique geology. A nature trail identifies Mojave plants.

DIRECTIONS: Trailheads are located at both the campground and information center (open from October through April on Wednesday through Sunday and from May through September, Saturdays only).

THE HIKE: From the Information Center, walk the wide path and look for signs displaying the names of cacti and other desert flora. At the campground, the trail narrows, bends left to the picnic area, and goes left again to join the gravel road for the return to the trailhead.

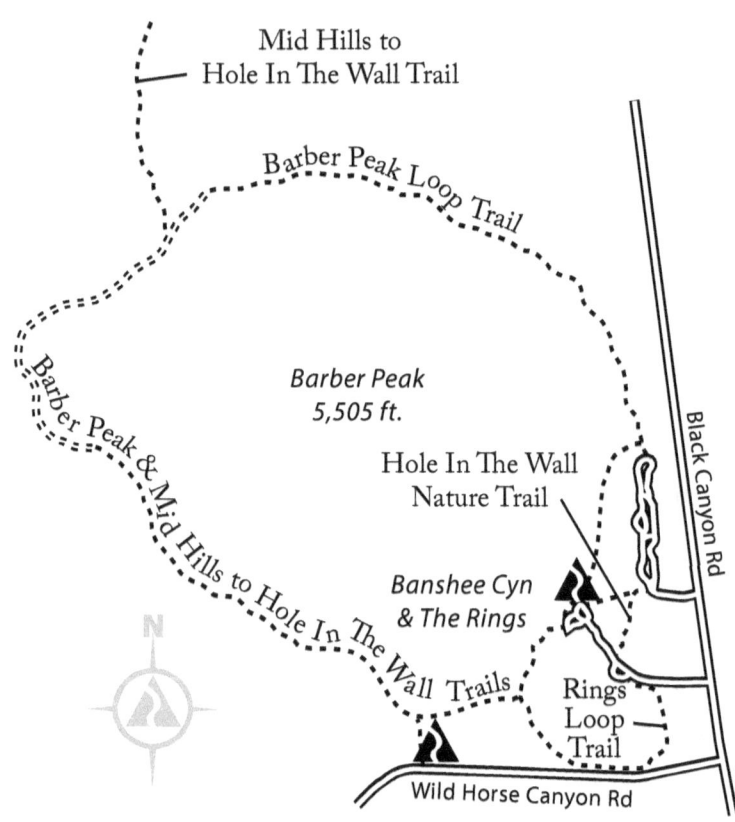

Barber Peak

Barber Peak Loop Trail

6 mile loop

Longest and most ambitious of the trio of trails at Hole-in-the-Wall, Barber Peak Trail loops around the 5,505-foot peak (more of a mesa, really) located just west of the campground. The path crosses cattle country and tours the Opalite Cliffs, an impressive castle-like formation, then returns to the campground and trailhead via Banshee Canyon.

Hikers have long been attracted to Hole-in-the-Wall. But the Rings Trail, however compelling, is short and the Mid Hills to Hole-in-the-Wall jaunt is a long one-way and requires shuttle logistics. The trail circling Barber Peak (Barber Butte on some maps) is not too short, not too long, and may be the just the right hike for you.

In 2007, volunteer trail builders (hats off to the Volunteer Vacations crew from the American Hiking Society!) and NPS staff constructed 3 miles of new trail that linked existing paths to fashion Barber Peak Loop Trail.

Trail-builders figured campers would be the ones to use the trail and the trailhead was placed at the campground; however, day hikers proved to be the chief users of the trail and most were baffled about where to park and how to join the path. NPS recently constructed a bypass trail and now the loop can be completed without tramping through the campground.

Along with the trail's considerable charms, two four-letter words are associated with this hike: cows and fire.

Remember, the primary difference between a national park and a national preserve is that a preserve allows grazing. You might hike past some cows and a lot of cow pies on this trail. The hiker passes through barbed wire fencing in ways humans can and cows can't: via narrow zigzags and gates that latch. Personally, I've never minded encountering cattle on my sojourns—Point Reyes National Seashore and BLM lands all over the West come to mind.

The 2005 Hackberry Fire scorched the Hole-in-the-Wall environs. You might be thinking: "It's a desert. What can burn?"

Turns out, a lot. The death toll on trees is particularly obvious to the hiker: Joshua Trees, juniper and pinyon pine.

DIRECTIONS: (same as Rings Trail)

THE HIKE: Begin this counter-clockwise jaunt by hiking north, at first paralleling Black Canyon Road. Look out northeast toward Table Mountain, a 6,176-foot mesa that juts up from the desert floor.

Hike past the cliff faces at the base of Barber Peak as the trail bends west across a cactus-dotted floodplain. Signs on stakes keep you on track.

About halfway into the hike, the trail continues as a 4-wheel drive road. After passing a junction with northbound Mid Hills to Hole-in-the-Wall Trail, the road bends south near the Opalite Cliffs. Past the light-colored formations topped with black lava, the road ends and the footpath resumes, angling southeast.

For a grand finale, the path loops east into the mouth of Banshee Canyon. Ascend the Rings Trail back to the trailhead.

Barber Peak Trail offers hikers a longer exploration of Hole-in-the-Wall.

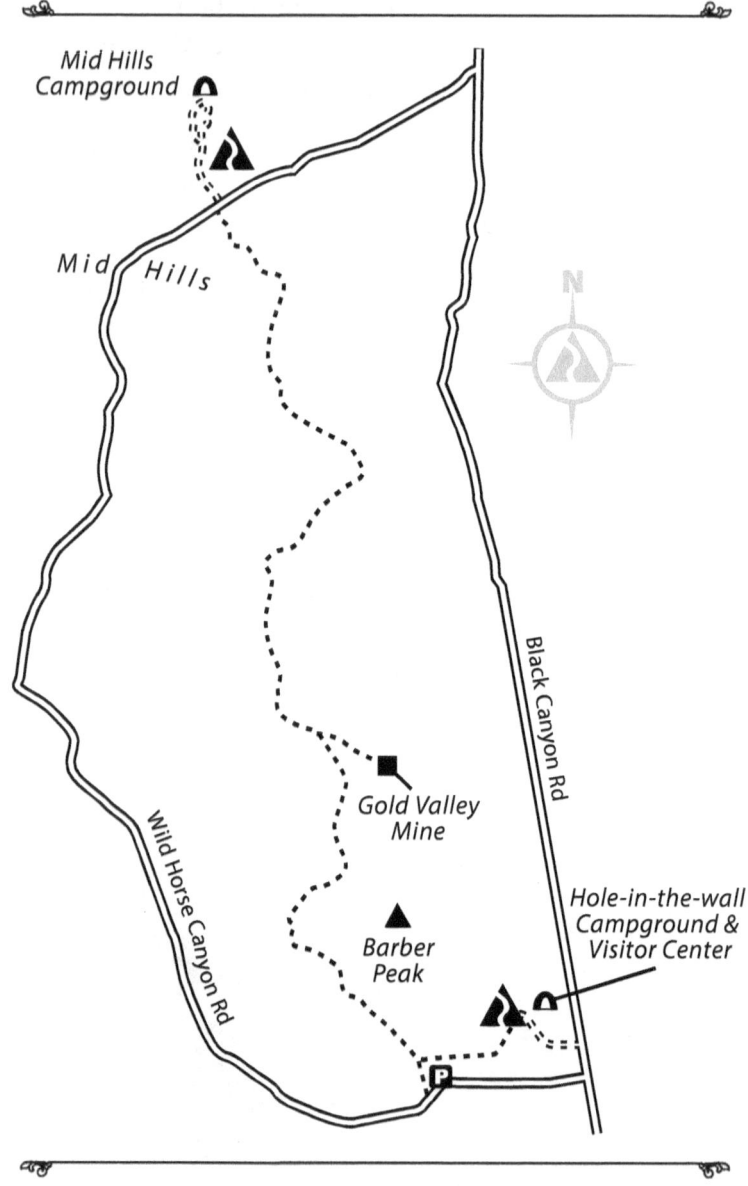

Mid Hills to Hole-in-the-Wall

Mid Hills to Hole-in-the-Wall Trail

From Mid Hills Campground to Hole-in-the-Wall Campground is 8 miles one-way with 1,200-foot elevation loss

Hole-in-the-Wall and Mid Hills are the centerpieces of Mojave National Preserve. Both locales offer diverse desert scenery and fine campgrounds. Doubling the pleasure of these special places is an 8-mile trail that connects them.

Mile-high Mid Hills recalls the Great Basin Desert topography. It's 1,000 or so feet higher than Hole-in-the-Wall and thus as a starting point offers the hiker an easier way to go. Some hikers, though, prefer beginning with that MNP highlight—the descent via Rings Trail into Hole-in-the-Wall. Coming or going, you'll traverse land recovering from the 2005 Hackberry Fire.

Mid Hills, named for its location halfway between the Providence and New York Mountains, offers a grand observation point from which to gaze out at MNP's dominant mountain ranges: the coffee-with-cream colored Pinto Mountains to the north, and the rolling Kelso Dunes shining on the western horizon.

Some of the route travels the bottom of sandy washes instead of over more clearly defined trails. Pay attention to NPS route markers.

The hike is an adventurous excursion through a diverse desert environment. You'll see basin and range tabletop mesas, encounter large pinyon trees, an array of colorful cactus and lichen-covered granite rocks. And views, views, views: Table Mountain, Wild Horse Mesa and the Providence Range.

DIRECTIONS: From Black Canyon Road, take the signed turnoff for Mid Hills Campground. Drive two miles to the Mid Hills trailhead located adjacent to a windmill immediately opposite the entrance road to the campground. The Hole-in-the-Wall trailhead is at the lip of Banshee Canyon.

THE HIKE: From the trailhead, the path ascends about 0.4 mile to a saddle, which offers splendid views of the Pinto Valley to the northeast. (The saddle is this hike's high point.)

From the saddle, the path angles south. Pass a gate about 1.2 mile from the trailhead and then descend into and climb out of a wash. (Keep a close eye on the trail; it's easy to lose here.) A bit more than 3 miles out, pass another signed fence.

After a modest ascent, the trail continues south to a minor pass and great views to the south of the Providence Mountains and Wild Horse Mesa.

At about the hike's halfway point, the trail passes through a gate and crosses the road to the Gold Valley Mine, where there's a working windmill. Continue south as the trail descends a dusty ridge then follows a wash for a mile.

Six miles out, the trail/old four-wheel road passes near the Opalite Cliffs Past the light-colored formations topped with black lava, the road ends and the footpath resumes, angling southeast.

For a grand finale, the path loops east into the mouth of Banshee Canyon. Ascend Rings Trail to Hole-in-the-Wall trailhead.

The Providence Mountains range rises to 7,162 feet and is home to Mitchell Caverns.

EVERY TRAIL TELLS A STORY.

III
Providence Mountains

HIKE ON.

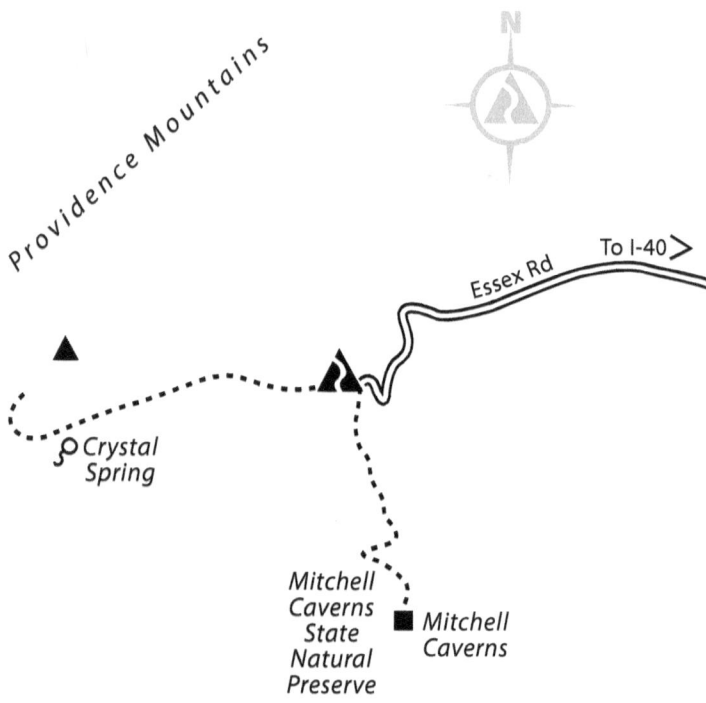

MITCHELL CAVERNS STATE RESERVE

MITCHELL CAVERNS TRAIL

1-mile guided hike of the caverns

Trail trivia question: Where can explore stunning scenery, be assured that it won't rain, and know that the temperature for your hike will always be a comfortable 65 degrees?

Hint: One of the overlooked gems of the California state park system.

If you're in the dark, then you're on the right path—the trail through Mitchell Caverns State Reserve, part of Providence Mountains State Recreation Area. Ranger-led walks through the dramatic limestone caves offer a fascinating geology lesson, one the whole family can enjoy.

In 1932, Jack Mitchell abandoned his Depression-shattered business in Los Angeles and moved to the desert. For a time he prospected for silver, but his real fascination was with what he called the "Providence" or "Crystal Caves" and their potential as a tourist attraction. He constructed several stone buildings to use for lodging. (Today's park visitors center is one of these buildings.) Mitchell and his wife Ida provided food, lodging, and guided tours of the caverns until 1954. By all accounts, Jack Mitchell was quite a yarn-spinner.

Now that the caverns are part of the state park system, rangers lead the tours. They're an enthusiastic lot and quite informative.

Walk through the two main caves, which Mitchell named El Pakiva (The Devil's House) and Tecopa (after a Shoshonean chieftain) and get close-up views of stalactites and stalagmites, cave ribbon, cave spaghetti and flow stone. And learn about some of the caverns' former inhabitants—the Chemehuevi Indians and a Pleistocene ground sloth that stumbled into the darkness some 15,000 years ago.

During Jack Mitchell's day, visitors had to be nimble rock-climbers who waited for their tour leader to toss flares into the darkness. Nowadays, the caverns are equipped with stairs and special lighting.

Providence Mountains SRA is open Friday-Sunday and holiday Mondays. From October-May, Mitchell Caverns tours are conducted at 11 AM and 2 PM; from June-September at 10 AM. More info: 760-928-2586.

DIRECTIONS: From Interstate Highway 40, about 80 miles east of Barstow, exit on Essex Road and drive 16 miles to road's end at the Providence Mountains State Recreation Area parking lot. Sign up at the visitor center for tours.

THE HIKE: Because you can only tour the caverns with a park ranger, and because you wouldn't want me to spoil the many surprises of the cave walk with a step-by-step description, I won't further detail the tour of Mitchell Caverns. After exploring "the great indoors" the park's outdoors pathways.

Explore the Great Indoors on a guided tour of the limestone caves of Mitchell Caverns.

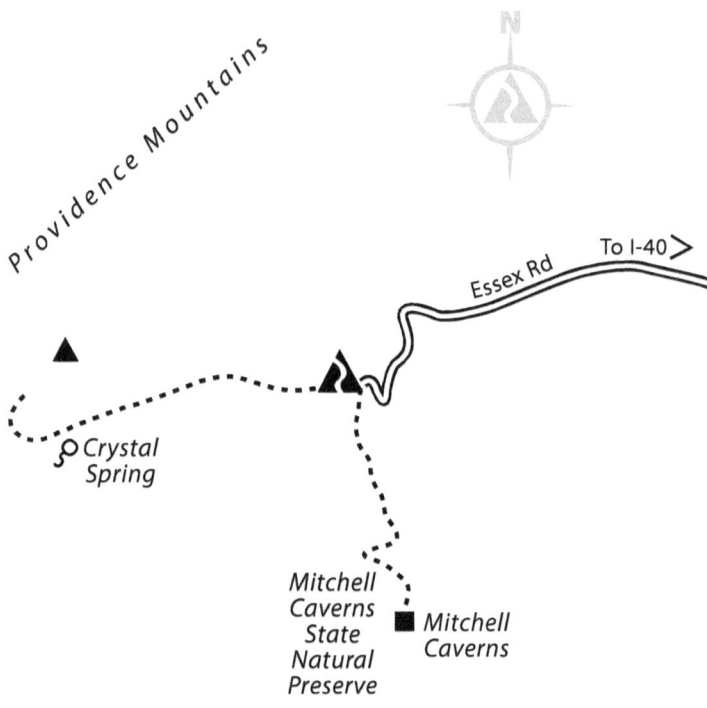

Providence Mountains

Crystal Spring Trail

From Mitchell Caverns to Crystal Spring is 2 miles round tip with 600-foot elevation gain

Crystal Springs Trail leads into the pinyon pine- and juniper dotted Providence Mountains by way of Crystal Canyon. Bighorn sheep often travel through this canyon.

Crystal Canyon is walled with limestone and rhyolite, a red volcanic rock. High above the canyon, castle-like formations of this rhyolite crown the Providence Mountains.

The steep and rather rocky trail offers an exploration of an inviting high desert canyon, engaging vistas of the spires of Providence Mountains peaks, and far-reaching views all the way to the Hualapai Mountains in Arizona, 100 miles away.

Providence Mountains State Recreation Area is a 5,900-acre island of state parkland within the preserve's boundaries. With dramatic mile-high peaks as a backdrop, this area features a variety of plant communities, short hikes, a small campground, and ranger-led tours of one of the most intriguing limestone caves in the West.

This state parkland is a must-see detour for MNP visitors. As you travel north on Essex Road, you'll see the massive Providence Mountains looming to the northwest. The highest peaks in the range are 6,996-foot Fountain Peak and 7,171-foot Edgar Peak, both located just west of the visitor center.

The Providence Mountains, limestone peaks intermixed with ancient volcanic, sedimentary and crystalline formations, are among Mojave's tallest mountains. They rise above the Clipper Valley and Kelso Basin; the west end forms a 600-foot escarpment—one of the most prominent views in this land of basin and range faulting.

During the 1880s, the Bonanza King Mine was a major source of silver in the area. The town of Providence was founded by the miners; its population hovered around 500 until mine operations ceased in 1887. More than $60 million dollars worth of silver was mined from the legendary Bonanza King.

In 1954, the California state parks system purchased the caves and surrounding land from Ida Mitchell, the widow of Jack Mitchell who developed the area and the caverns that bear his name.

DIRECTIONS: (*Park subject to closure.* Call 760-928-2586) From I-40, about 80 miles east of Barstow, exit on Essex Road and drive 16 miles to road's end Join the signed trail ascending the slope near the stone visitor center.

THE HIKE: In less than 0.25 mile, ascend into a unique landscape framed by bold rhyolite outcroppings. Pinyon pine join a veritable cactus garden of barrel, cholla and prickly-pear cacti.

About 0.5 mile out, look for the pipeline Jack Mitchell built in the 1930s to supply his tourist attraction in-the-making. The path crosses to the canyon's right side and continues a last 0.25 mile to the end of the trail, just short of willow-screened Crystal Spring. Proceed on fainter trail to the spring and on to a viewpoint a short distance beyond.

The view of Clipper Valley to the east extends 100 open miles. To put that distance in perspective, consider that the entire Los Angeles Basin would fit into the empty valley below!

Mary Beal dedicated herself to gathering, classifying and preserving the region's desert flora.

TheTrailmaster.com

Mary Beal's Mojave
Nature Trail

0.5 mile round trip

Mary Beal Nature Trail offers a great introduction to high desert flora. Cliffrose and blue sage share the hillsides with cholla, catclaw and creosote.

The trail honors Mary Beal, a Riverside librarian "exiled" to the desert by her doctor for health reasons. For a half-century this remarkable woman wandered remote Mojave Desert locales gathering and classifying hundreds of varieties of wildflowers and other plants. The trail was dedicated in 1952 on Beal's seventy-fifth birthday.

DIRECTIONS: Walk the road north of the visitor center to the signed start of the trail.

THE HIKE: The path meanders an alluvial plain. Prickly pear, cholla and assorted yuccas spike surrounding slopes. Benches offer restful places from which to contemplate cacti, admire volcanic boulders and count roadrunners.

Teutonia Peak Trail, seen here before a 2020 wildfire, leads to grand views of Cima Dome and far beyond.

EVERY TRAIL TELLS A STORY.

IV

Ivanpah Valley

HIKE ON.

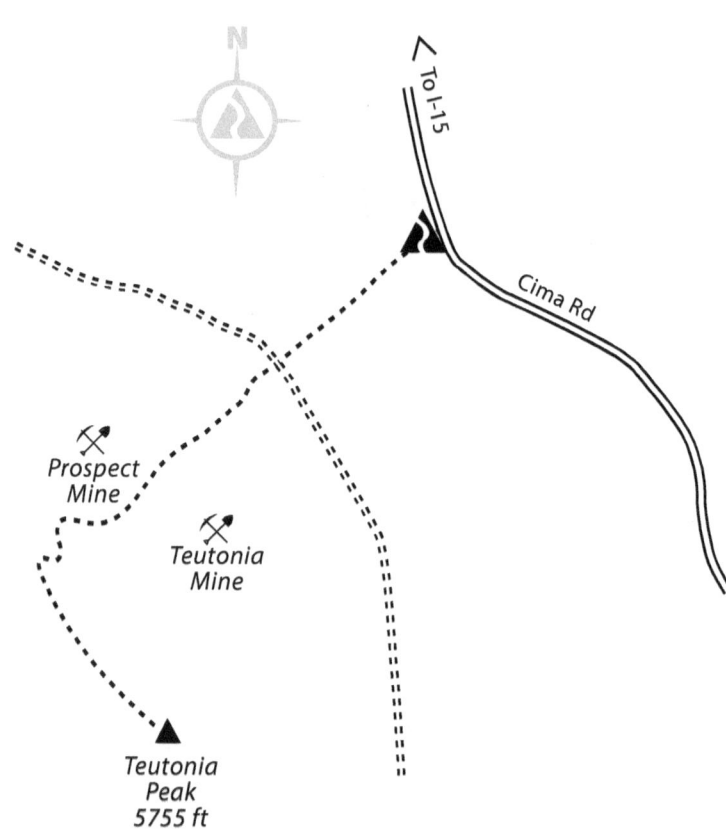

Cima Dome
Teutonia Peak Trail

To Teutonia Peak, is 4 miles round trip

Cima Dome is certainly one of the easiest Mojave National Preserve sights to reach, but when you reach it, you may wonder why you did. It's not a geologic formation you can view close-up: the Dome slopes so gently, it's best viewed from a distance. What Gertrude Stein said of Oakland comes to mind: "There's no there there."

Two places to get "the big picture" of Cima Dome are from Mid Hills Campground and from I-15 as you drive southeast of Baker and crest a low rise. And another is from the summit of Teutonia Peak (elevation 5,755 feet), reached by a trail that crosses a stellar Joshua Tree woodland and ascends a steep yucca- and cactus-dotted slope.

Cima Dome is a mass of once-molten monzonite, a granite-like rock. Over thousands of years it's been extensively eroded and now sprawls over some 75 square miles. It's more than 10 miles in diameter.

Another distinctive feature of the dome is its handsome rock outcroppings—the same type found in Joshua Tree National Park to the south. Rock climbers, rock scramblers, and hikers love Cima's rock show.

The word to remember around Cima Dome is symmetry. A geological rarity, the formation has been called the most symmetrical natural dome in the U.S. Take a look at the area's USGS topographical map, study Cima's near-concentric contour lines, and you'll likely agree with this symmetry claim.

Cima's Joshua trees are tall—some more than 25 feet high—and several hundred years old. Unfortunately, the world's largest and densest Joshua tree forest was ravaged by a 2020 wildfire, one of the most horrific examples of climate change in the national park system. What's left of the woodland are Joshuas and junipers that survived amidst clusters of boulders, green islands on a brown land.

Teutonia Peak Trail offers a unique perspective on Cima Dome, which rises 1,500 feet above the surrounding desert playas. It's all the more appealing to hikers because it's an actual trail—as opposed to a route through a wash—and has been nicely upgraded over the years.

DIRECTIONS: From Interstate 15, exit on Cima Road and drive 11 miles south to the signed trailhead and parking area. (For north-bound travelers on Kelso-Cima Road, the trailhead is located 6.5 miles north of Cima Junction.)

THE HIKE: Begin with a mellow meander southwest thorough scorched Joshua tree forest to a gate at the 0.5-mile mark. Ascend another 0.5 mile to a left branching jeep trail that leads 0.25 mile to Teutonia Mine (collapsed wood structure, large mine shaft covered with a metal grate).

The path narrows and soon reaches the base of Teutonia Peak. Ascend rocky slopes amidst prickly pear cactus. Climb steeply on stone steps to a notch below the two prominent rock masses atop the peak. Enjoy grand views of Cima Dome from the lookout. From the lookout, experienced rock climbers can scramble 0.25 mile to the top of Teutonia Peak.

A 2020 desert wildfire devastated the Joshua tree forest around Cima Dome. Heartbreaking.

What will the future bring for Hotel Nipton and the town of Nipton (shuttered at this writing)?

TheTrailmaster.com

NIPTON

NIPTON WALKABOUT

Around town is 0.25 mile round trip

Located just two miles from the California/Nevada border, Nipton's town motto is "Where the past is present." It's perfectly appropriate, especially when freight trains rumble through.

Geologist Jerry Freeman purchased the town in 1984, restored the store and Hotel Nipton, and created an off-the-beaten path gateway to MNP.

DIRECTIONS: From Interstate 15, some 40 miles east of Baker and some 10 miles west of the California/Nevada border, exit on Nipton Road and travel 10 miles east to the hamlet of Nipton.

THE HIKE: Check out the Nipton Trading Post then stroll past old buildings, Hotel Nipton, and railroad tracks extending to infinity. At night, see the lights of Las Vegas; better yet, all the stars in the Universe sparkling in the sky.

Take a drive—and hike—to the unique beauties of the New York Mountains.

EVERY TRAIL TELLS A STORY.

V
NEW YORK MOUNTAINS

HIKE ON.

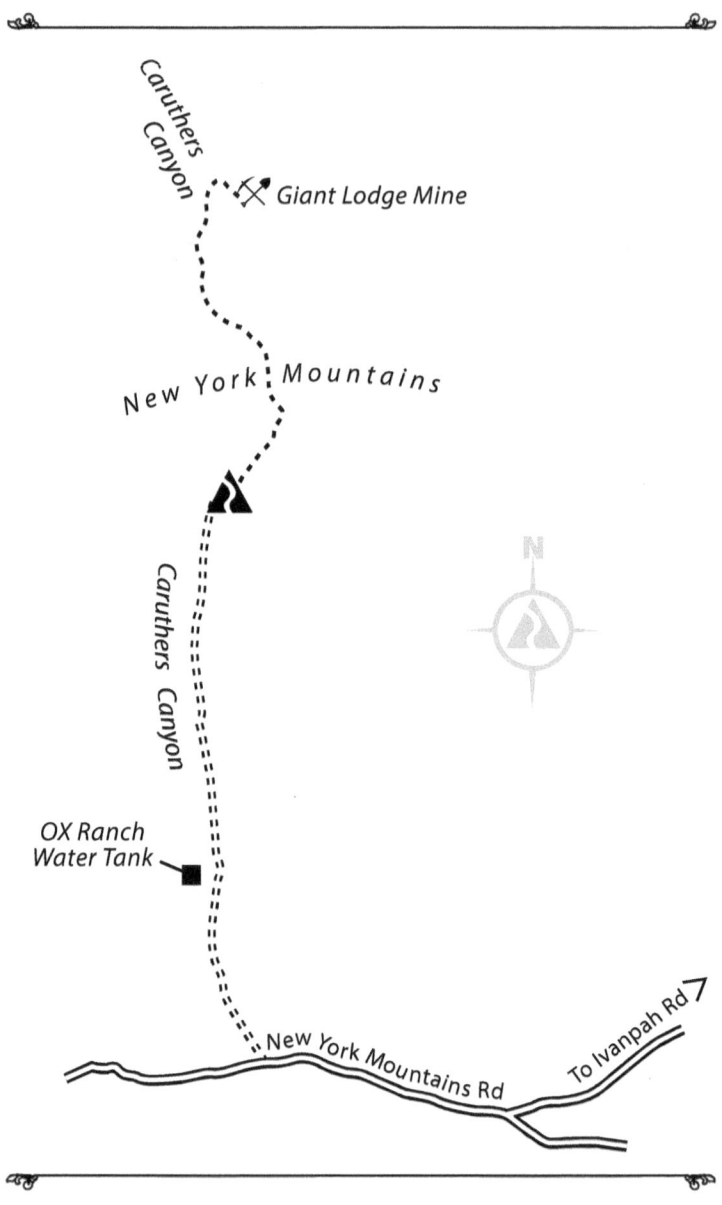

CARUTHERS CANYON

CARUTHERS CANYON TRAIL

From Caruthers Canyon to Giant Ledge Mine is 3 miles round trip with 400-foot elevation gain

Botanists call them disjuncts. Bureaucrats call them UPAs (Unusual Plant Assemblages). The more lyrical naturalists among us call them islands on the land.

By whatever name, the isolated communities of pinyon pine and white fir in the New York Mountains are very special places. Nearly 300 plant species have been counted on the slopes of this range and in its colorfully named canyons.

Perhaps the most botanically unique area in the mountains, indeed in the whole Mojave National Preserve, is Caruthers Canyon. A cool, inviting pinyon pine-juniper woodland stands in marked contrast to more sparsely vegetated parts of the desert. The conifers are joined by oaks and a variety of coastal chaparral plants including manzanita, yerba santa, ceanothus and coffee berry.

What is a coastal ecosystem doing in the middle of the desert?

Botanists believe that during wetter times such coastal scrub vegetation was quite widespread. As the climate became more arid, coastal ecosystems were "stranded" atop high and moist slopes. The botanical islands high in the New York Mountains are outposts of Rocky Mountains and coastal California flora.

Bird-watchers spot the western tanager, gray-headed junco, yellow-breasted chat and many more species. High in the sky are golden eagles, prairie falcons and red-tailed hawks.

Caruthers Canyon is a treat for the hiker. A dirt road, deteriorating into a footpath, leads through a rocky basin full of golden-hued granite boulders and into a historic mining region. Prospectors began digging in the New York Mountains in the 1860s and continued well into the 20th century. At trail's end are mine shafts and huge piles of tailings from Giant Ledge Mine, an abandoned copper mine.

DIRECTIONS: (High clearance vehicles necessary; four-wheel drive recommended.) From Ivanpah Road, turn west on New York Mountains Road (a couple OX Cattle Ranch buildings stand near this road's intersection) and drive 5.5 miles to an unsigned junction with a dirt road. Turn north and proceed 2.7 miles to a woodland laced with turnouts that serve as unofficial campsites. Leave your vehicle here; farther along the road dips into a wash, gets very rough then impassable.

THE HIKE: From the Caruthers Canyon "Campground" follow the main dirt road up the canyon. As you ascend, look behind you for a great view of Table Mountain, the most dominant peak of the central part of Mojave.

Handsome boulders line the trail and frame views of the tall peak before you, New York Mountain. The range's 7,532-foot signature peak is crowned with a botanical island of its own—a relict stand of white fir.

About 0.8 mile along, dip in out of a wash a couple times and gain a great view of the canyon and its castellated walls. If it's rained recently, you might find water collected in pools on the rocky canyon bottom. Enjoy the tranquility of the mine area, but don't stray into dangerous shafts.

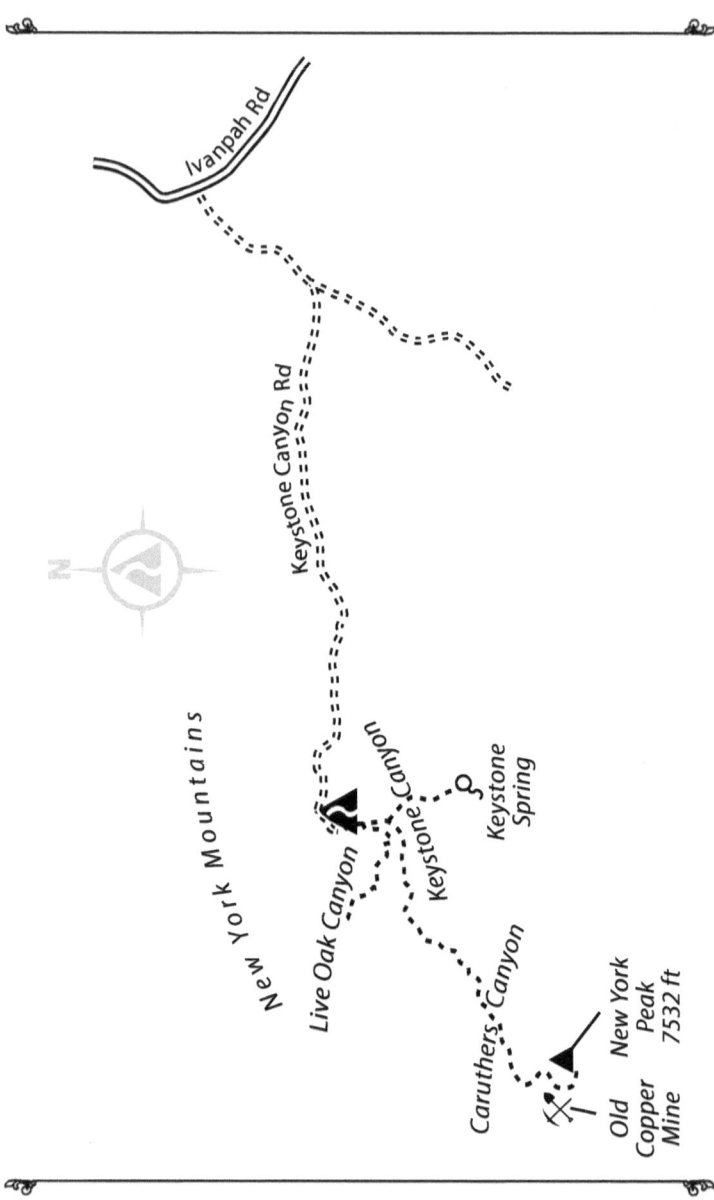

Keystone Canyon & New York Peak

Keystone Canyon Trail

From Keystone Canyon to road's end is 3 miles round trip with 700-foot elevation gain; to New York Peak is 7 miles round trip with a 2,300-foot gain

Thrusting high above Lanfair Valley, the impressive, granite-crowned New York Mountains are among the preserve's highest peaks. New York Peak, the range's 7,463-foot signature summit, offers commanding views of the preserve and far beyond.

Northeast of the peak lies Keystone Canyon, botanically similar to Caruthers Canyon, located a few miles to the south. Both canyons cradle relict stands of white fir—arboreal survivors from a time of much cooler and wetter climatic conditions.

Yerba santa, ceanothus and other shrubs more common to California's coastal slopes grow in the upper reaches of the New York Mountains. Lower Keystone Canyon hosts pinyon pine, juniper and turbinella oak. More typical preserve vegetation such as Mojave yucca, sagebrush and prickly pear are also a strong presence in the canyon.

Seasoned hikers with good route-finding skills can tackle the steep and challenging ascent to New York Peak. Add another 4 miles round trip (and 1,500 feet more elevation gain) of hiking to reach the summit.

DIRECTIONS: (High clearance vehicle required and four-wheel drive recommended for road into Keystone Canyon.) From Interstate 15, exit on Nipton Road and travel 3.5 miles to Ivanpah Road. Turn right (south) and head 12 miles to Ivanpah, where the road crosses railroad tracks, bends east, and turns to dirt. After 6 more miles, as Ivanpah Road bends southeast, turn right on the narrow, unsigned road leading to Keystone Canyon. Avoid left-forking, narrower roads, travel 2.7 miles up deteriorating road, and park just before the road crosses a wash.

THE HIKE: Crisscross the wash a few times as the old road heads south. Trailside flora includes pinyon pine and juniper, yerba santa and cliffrose.

About 0.75 mile out, note a right-forking road that leads into Live Oak Canyon (well worth exploring). A bit more than a mile out, spot an old water pipe and left-forking trail that leads 0.25 mile to Keystone Spring.

Continue the ascent as views of granite-topped mountains improve and the road you're following deteriorates. At road's end, find a small abandoned copper mine. It's colorful in an odd sort of way—green and blue copper ore debris scattered around ore car tracks that protrude from the mine shaft.

From the mine, skilled mountaineers ascend the steep wash, and work their way up to a ridgeline and narrow saddle. Then it's another stiff ascent to reach the ridgecrest just south of New York Peak. Scramble southwest among the boulders.

It's a Class 3 climb to reach the highest rocky pinnacle known as New York 2. Otherwise, enjoy the marvelous view from the ridge: Cima Dome to the west and Clark Mountain to the northwest, the high peaks of the San Bernardino and San Gabriel mountains, and on really clear days the Virgin Mountains of far southwestern Utah, located more than a 100 miles to the northeast.

*Get your kicks—and take a few hikes—
along Route 66.*

EVERY TRAIL TELLS A STORY.

V
OFF ROUTE 66

HIKE ON.

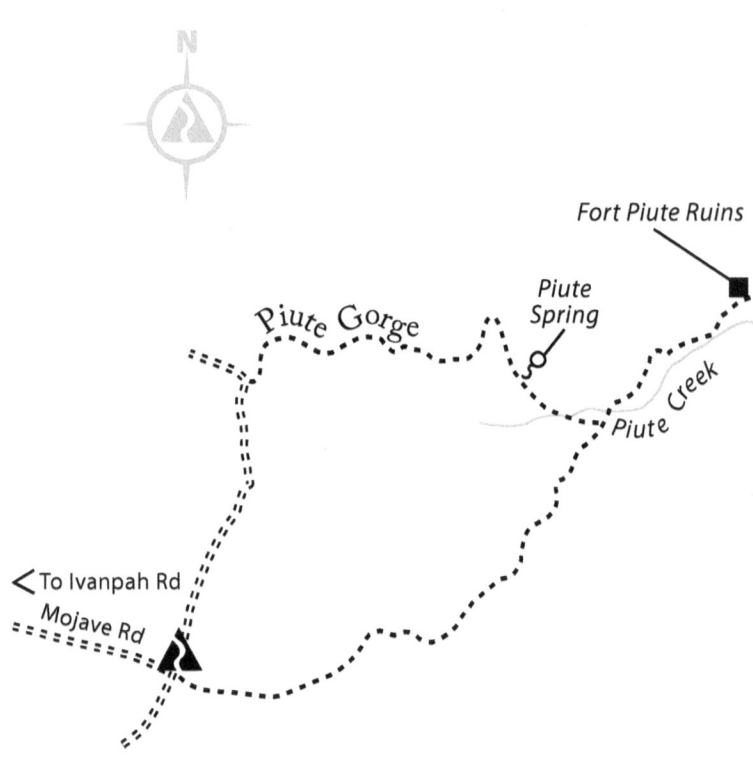

PIUTE CANYON

OLD MOJAVE ROAD, PIUTE CANYON TRAILS

To Fort Piute and return via Piute Gorge is 7 miles round trip with 600-foot elevation gain

In 1865, Fort Piute was described by a visitor as "a Godforsaken place—the meanest I ever saw for a military station." Few would disagree; however, the ruins of the fort, along with the old Mojave Road and an ascent through impressive Piute Gorge add up to a way off-the-beaten-path hike to remember.

The fort was established to protect pioneer travelers on their westward journeys. Today the small, primitive installation lies in ruins, its thick rock and mortar walls weathered and crumbled to a height of just two or three feet. Stone outlines delineate rooms that served as living quarters, corral and cookhouse.

Another hike highlight: Piute Creek, the only perennial stream in MNP, is an oasis-like area where cottonwoods, willows and sedges flourish. The walls of Piute Gorge soar 600 feet above the canyon floor, which narrows in places to only 10 feet wide.

DIRECTIONS: (Four-wheel drive recommended) From I-40, take the Fenner/Essex turnoff and head 10 miles east on Route 66 to the hamlet of Goffs. Turn left Lanfair Road and drive 16 miles to a point about 100 feet beyond its junction with Cedar Canyon Road. Turn right (east) on "Cable Road" (AT&T cable route). Stay right at a junction 3.7 miles out, and stick with the cable road 6 more miles to another junction where there's a cattle guard. Turn left before the cattleguard on a sketchy dirt road and go north 0.5 mile to an abandoned section of the Mojave Road and a parking area.

THE HIKE: Trek east to the top of a saddle at Piute Hill and pause to take in the view: Table Mountain to the west, Castle Peaks to the north. The rocky route descends a difficult grade that challenged pioneers and their wagons. A mile from the trailhead, the eroded road drops into a wash, 2 miles out passes petroglyphs on pale red rocks, and shortly thereafter crosses Piute Creek.

Note Piute Canyon Trail coming in from the west, but instead join the path on the north bank of the creek and descend northeast 0.5 mile to the ruins of Fort Piute.

Tour (but don't disturb) the remains of "Fort Pah Ute, 1867-68," then head back on Mojave Road 0.5 mile, bearing right on unsigned Piute Canyon Trail.

Piute Canyon

This narrow path stays high on the canyon wall, heading west at first, then north. A half-mile along, glimpse prominent Piute Gorge.

Stick with the faint cairn-way-marked path continuing westward. Reach the mouth of the gorge at the 4-mile mark, descend a side canyon to the main gorge and for the next 1.5 miles enjoy a stirring descent over sandy terrain with a variety of volcanic rock walling you off from the world. Desert hiking—as good as it gets!

Exiting the gorge, follow a cairn-marked route 0.5 mile to meet a dirt road. Follow the road south along the base of the Piute Hills, passing a corral, for 1 mile back to the trailhead.

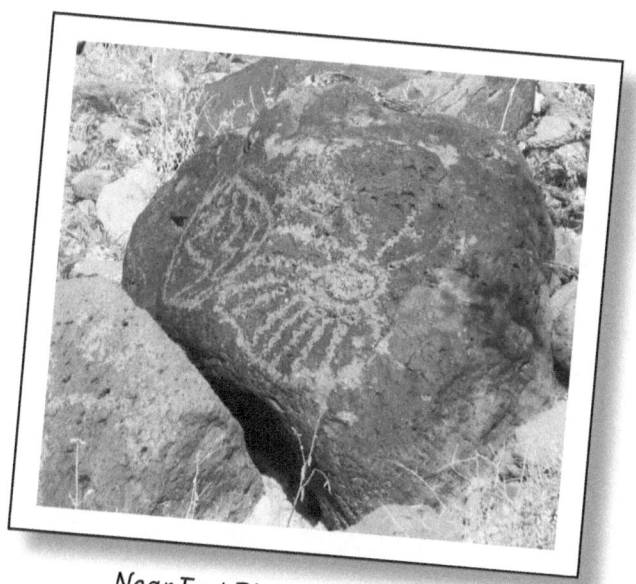

Near Fort Piute, look for Native American petroglyphs.

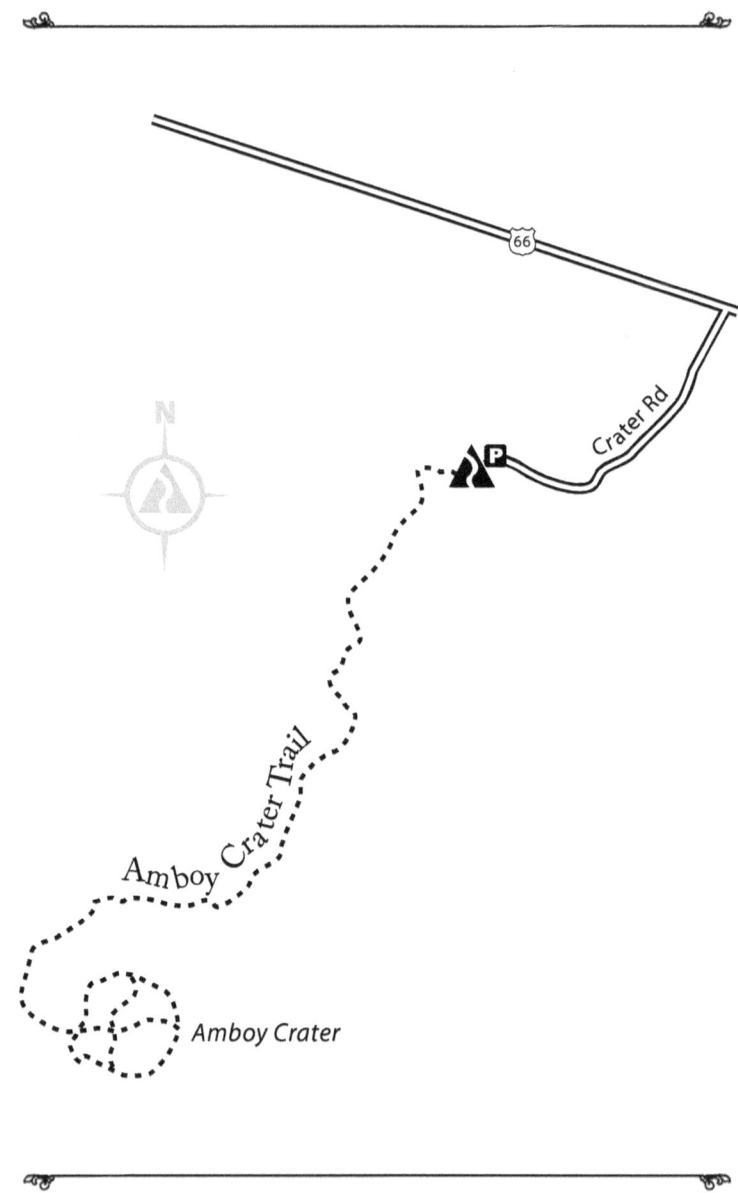

AMBOY CRATER

AMBOY CRATER TRAIL

3 miles round trip with 200-foot elevation gain

We're fascinated by volcanoes and, as long as they're not too hot and not active, we like to visit them. Amboy Crater, located out in the eastern Mojave Desert with the old-time diners and abandoned gas stations along historic old Route 66, long been a curiosity for generations of desert travelers.

The little volcano can be reached with a short hike, an ideal leg-stretcher for motorists desiring a break from interminable Interstate 40. In 1973, the same year I-40 opened and diverted almost all traffic from Route 66, Amboy Crater and its lava field were designated Amboy Crater National Natural Landmark. BLM has improved access to the crater and added restrooms, a picnic area and crater viewing platform.

Getting to the volcano's trailhead via Route 66 can be thoroughly enjoyable. The stretch of Route 66 from just outside Barstow to just west of Needles is the longest and best-preserved stretch of the historic route in California.

Amboy Crater was a popular sight-to-see along old Route 66. However, many travelers were repelled, not attracted, by this scene. In *The Grapes of Wrath*, John Steinbeck wrote: "And 66 goes on over the terrible desert, where the distance shimmers and the black cinder mountains hang unbearably in the distance."

About 28 miles east of Ludlow, look for extensive Hawaiian-like lava fields. Amboy Crater, which erupted 10,000 years ago (some accounts peg its eruption at just 500 years ago), is the cause of this flow, and lies just south of the road. Amboy Crater and environs are covered with two kinds of lava: *aa* (pronounced ah-ah), sharp, hiking boot-assaulting hunks of basalt and *pahoehoe* (pa-hoy-hoy), smoother, rope-like lava.

The town of Amboy, a few miles east of the crater, is noted for Roy's Motel & Café, popular with motorists during the Route 66 heyday. Gas and snacks are available here.

DIRECTIONS: From Ludlow, drive 28 miles southeast on Route 66 to just short of Amboy. Turn south on signed Crater Road leading 0.5 mile to the parking lot, restrooms and observation deck for Amboy Crater. From I-40 at the southern boundary of Mojave NP, drive 11 miles south on Kelbaker Road to meet Route 66. Go west 5.8 miles to Amboy then another 1.8 miles to the turnoff for the crater.

THE HIKE: Follow the wide path, dotted with interpretive signs, which narrows to a trail and heads southwest across the desert floor. A mile out, the path bends around the right side of the crater and climbs rocky switchbacks to a wide opening in the crater rim and a junction with Crater and Rim trails.

Crater Trail leads into this breach in the cone, and across the center to the summit (elevation 944 feet) for panoramic vistas of the surrounding lavascape and the eastern Mojave. From here, hike Rim Trail in either direction to return to the junction and the trail back.

Amble out to Amboy Crater. It's not every day you get to visit a volcano.

Mojave National Preserve Stories

EVERY TRAIL TELLS A STORY.

From the Diary of Fr. Garcés
Father Francisco Hermenegildo Tomás Garcés was a Spanish Franciscan missionary and explorer, who traveling through what would become Mojave National Preserve in 1776.

Mar. 10. I went 6 leagues up the arroyo on a course west-southwest, and with various windings I halted in the same arroyo, at a place where it has cottonwoods, much grass, and lagunas.

Mar. 11. Having gone one league east-southeast I arrived at some rancherias so poor that they had to eat no other thing than the roots of rushes.

Mar. 12. I traveled two leagues west-southwest, and halted in the same arroyo [on the Mojave River], at an uninhabited rancheria; the rain, the cold, and hunger continued, for there were no roots of tule, and the remaining inhabited rancherias were afar. In which emergency I determined that my companions should kill a horse to relieve the necessity; not even was the blood thereof wasted, for indeed there was need to go on short rations in order to survive the days that we required to reach the next rancherias. On account of the severe cold turned back from here one Jamajab Indian of those who were accompanying me; of the other two Indians of his nation, I covered the one with a blanket, and the other with a shirt. As there was much to eat of the dead horse, they would not depart hence until the 15th day.

Mar 16. I traveled two leagues west-northwest. Then quitting the arroyo I traveled southwest until I fell into it again, and continued therein with some inclination to the south. Having gone four leagues I came to where there were good grass, large cottonwoods, cranes, and crows of the kind that there is at San Gabriel.

Mar. 17. At the passage of the river the mule mired down, and wetted was all that he was carrying, and for this did I tarry here. This day I dispatched one Jamajab and Sevastian, that they should seek the inhabited rancherias.

Father Francisco Garcés, missionary and explorer, trekked across the Mojave in 1776.

"Hello Folks, This is Curtis Springer…"

"The Reverend Doctor" Curtis Springer, who was neither a reverend nor a doctor, but a canny con man/radio evangelist, broadcast from his studio in Zzyzx. The selection below, a sampling of his syndicated show, aired in 1944.

"Hello folks! This is your old friend Curtis Springer coming to you direct from our beautiful new studios located at Zzyzx Community Church on the shores of beautiful Lake Tuendae. And as founder and pastor of our church I want to invite you and your loved ones to come worship with us. Come with or without money and spend a day or a week or a lifetime as you care to and enjoy our beautiful 12,000-acre estate that belongs to God."

Doc Springer broadcasted to radio stations across the country from his studio in Zzyzx.

We have no promotion, no real estate for sale. Just come on out here and enjoy our wonderful hot mineral water baths, the finest of food in abundance, our wonderful desert pure fresh air—no smog no fog. Come and learn to breathe again! Lay out in the sunshine. Oh, you'll love it here. You'll get a greater joy out of life.

So until the same time tomorrow over the same wonderful radio station I'll say bye-bye, and God bless you all."

Railroad Man Buried In Desert
Apparently deciding to walk from Afton Canyon to Las Vegas wasn't the best idea. This news story was printed in the July 26, 1910 edition of the San Bernardino Sun.

Coroner C.D. Van Wie returned yesterday from Kelso where he went to hold an inquest upon the remains of Ben M. Banks, a railroad man who perished of heat on the desert last week. The deceased had been in the railroad employ at Kelso as a Salt Lake trainman. He rode with the wrecking crew from that point to Afton and had walked as far as Balch, a distance of 22 miles through the glaring sun, perishing just before reaching Balch.

After the inquest, Banks was given a picturesque burial. His hearse was a locomotive. The casket was placed on the cowcatcher, and the mourners crowded into the cab and found a place to ride wherever there was foothold. The engine was run out onto the desert some distance and there all that was mortal of Ben banks was buried, railroad honors being accorded the deceased, who had perished while trying to foot it to Las Vegas.

If This Land Could Speak
Cheri Rae writes movingly of the East Mojave in this excerpt from the first edition of *East Mojave Desert: A Visitors Guide* (Olympus Press, 1989)

If this land could speak, what stories it would tell! Tales of Indians and Spanish explorers, trappers and trailblazers, pioneers and gold miners, cattle ranchers, and restless spirits. It would speak of the past when rugged individualists and determined families lived harmoniously with this place working hard with their hands, traversing it quietly, carefully, with a little fear and a lot of respect, and leaving behind little more than tracks in the sand. It would tell of booms and busts, lone prospectors, and great armies, those who scratched at the land and scarred it, those who lived with the land and loved it.

If this land could speak it would remind us, we last minute arrivals on the scene, that it has witnessed profound changes in form and substance, change by firestorm and flood and the passage of millions of years. It would speak of the great oceans and tropical forests that once covered it and speak of the cactus and creosote, jimson and juniper, and the thousand

and one living things that bloom and blossom and cover it today. It would speak of the great numbers of animals that have inhabited this place—some now extinct, others whose very existence is endangered.

Yet this land that cannot speak calls to us. Some of us have been drawn to its silent places, some of us have let the desert fill our hearts. It's a call of the wild that can't be heard, only felt and experienced.

"If you would experience a landscape, you must go alone into it and sit down somewhere quietly and wait for it to come in its own good time to you," writes Paul Gruchow in *The Necessity of Empty Places*. I propose that you visit some of the silent places of Mojave National Preserve and take your own sweet time of it.

When the land speaks to you and you are moved—and you will be moved because no one who visits the wonders of this desert land is left unmoved—you, too, will want to speak for the land. And when you speak, I hope it is with a clear voice, a strong voice, a voice that speaks from the heart of the beauty you have seen and of the necessity for preserving this beauty in a world that has already lost far too many wild, beautiful, silent places

Our New 'Crown Jewel' is Trashed

In response to a local Congressman who succeeded cutting off funding for the newly created Mojave National Preserve, John McKinney blasted him in an editorial published in the *Los Angeles Times* on June 28, 1995.

Millions of Americans, along with travelers from around the world, will visit California desert parks and preserves this year and they will spend millions of dollars doing so. A national park, like a professional sports team, brings prestige, a high profile, and significant revenue to the region in which it's located.

This economic fact of life is lost on Rep. Jerry Lewis (R-Redlands) who cannot see any value—economic ecological or spiritual—in California desert parks and actually wants to wipe one of them off the map.

If Lewis, long a champion of off-road vehicle users, hunters and mining interests, has his way, the newly created Mojave National Preserve would be no more. The crown jewel of the California desert a 1.4-million-acre wonderland of vast sand dunes, dramatic geologic formations, a dozen mountain ranges and the world's largest Joshua tree forest, would be stripped from the stewardship of the National Park Service.

While smart politicians generally take a you-win-some-you-lose-some approach Lewis and fellow grumps who took their lumps after passage of last year's landmark California Desert Protection Act are still fighting desert preservation this time by choking off funding.

There's magic and money in the words *national park*. Millions of tourist dollars are left behind in and around gateway towns outside national parks, and the towns near Southern California's desert parks are no exception. Already Death Valley National Park, Joshua Tree National Park and Mojave National Preserve have become a national and international tourism magnet as the "three desert parks tour." In Baker, gateway to the Mojave National Preserve, the conversant-in-a-dozen-languages staff of the Mad Greek restaurant even offers foreign newspapers for customers to peruse. Occupancy at the Hotel Nipton in the northeast corner of the preserve has increased 80% from pre preserve days.

No wonder business owners and officials in eastern San Bernardino County where the preserve is located have appealed to Lewis to stop his park-bashing. Nevertheless, even as a House committee was committing another environmental atrocity by trying to lift California's offshore drilling ban, Lewis succeeded in scrapping the $600,000 that the National Park Service needs to set up a visitor center and for patrolling the Mojave reserve. On Tuesday, the full Appropriations Committee voted on the preserve's allocation for fiscal 1996: it will get $1.

This is not only mean spirited; it's also potentially dangerous. In the remote Mojave Desert, a well-staffed visitor center is essential to the safety of people exploring the preserve. A strong park service presence is also required for law enforcement and to protect resources from irresponsible users.

Lewis says the Park Service has been "hassling people" a claim that strains credibility considering that there is exactly 1 permanent field Ranger assigned to Mojave National Preserve. At a time when anti-government extremists are threatening rangers and public lands managers elsewhere in the West, Lewis and his fellow sore losers should watch what they say.

National parks remain one of the most revered institutions of modern American life, widely admired around the world. Most Americans, even the most fiscally conservative ones, would be embarrassed by the situation in the new Mojave preserve: park service seasonal employees and their families living in substandard housing and a park without a visitor center or even a decent map.

Even if certain Congress members cannot hear the silent symphony of the desert or appreciate the beauty of its composition, they should at least listen when money talks and cash registers ring. Mojave National Preserve must have its funds restored; then it must be upgraded to national park status so that Lewis and other politicos deaf to the desert music and blind to its beauty keep their hands off our public lands.

Death Valley NP
LAVA BEDS NM
YOSEMITE NATIONAL PARK
Joshua Tree National Park
Pinnacles NP
EUGENE O'NEILL NHS
MUIR WOODS NM
Whiskeytown-Shasta Trinity NRA
Golden Gate National Recreation Area
DEVILS POSTPILE NM
LASSEN VOLCANIC NATIONAL PARK
Cabrillo NM
REDWOOD NP
CHANNEL ISLANDS NATIONAL PARK
MOJAVE NPRES
César Chávez NM
John Muir NHS
Rosie the Riveter NHS
Santa Monica Mountains NRA
POINT REYES NS
SEQUOIA-KINGS CANYON NATIONAL PARKS

California's National Parks

Other states have national parks with tall trees, high peaks, deep canyons, long seashores and vast deserts, but only California can claim all these grand landscapes within its boundaries.

California boasts nine national parks, the most in the nation. In addition, the state's national parklands include national recreation areas, national monuments, national historic parks, a national seashore and a national preserve.

The state features one of America's oldest national parks—Yosemite set aside in 1890—and one of its newest—César E. Chávez National Monument established in 2012.

Mere acreage does not a national park make, but California's national parks include the largest park in the contiguous U.S.—3.3-million acre Death Valley National Park. Yosemite (748,542 acres) and Joshua Tree (790,636 acres) are also huge by any park standards. Even such smaller parklands as Redwoods National Park and Pt. Reyes National Seashore are by no means small.

California and The National Park Idea

Not long after John Muir walked through Mariposa Grove and into the Yosemite Valley, California's natural treasures attracted attention worldwide and conservationists rallied to preserve them as parks. As the great naturalist put it in 1898: "Thousands of nerve-shaken, overcivilized people are beginning to find out that going to the mountains is going home; that wilderness is a necessity; and that mountain parks and reservations are useful not only as fountains of timber and irrigating rivers, but as fountains of life."

The National Park Service, founded in 1916, was initially guided by borax tycoon-turned-park-champion Stephen T. Mather and his young assistant, California attorney Horace Albright. The park service's mission was the preservation of "the scenery and the natural and historic objects and the wild life" and the provision "for the enjoyment of the same in such manner and by such means as will leave them unimpaired for the enjoyment of future generations."

The invention of the automobile revolutionized national park visitation, particularly in car-conscious California. John Muir called them "blunt-nosed mechanical beetles," yet as one California senator pointed out, "If Jesus Christ had an automobile he wouldn't have ridden a jackass into Jerusalem."

With cars came trailers, and with trailer camps came concessionaires. National parks filled with mobile cities of canvas and aluminum, and by visitors anxious to see California's natural wonders. During the 1920s and 30s, the park service constructed signs identifying scenic features and rangers assumed the role of interpreting nature for visitors.

By 1930 California had four national parks: Yosemite, Lassen, Sequoia and General Grant (Kings Canyon.) In the 1930s, two big desert areas—Joshua Tree and Death Valley—became national monuments.

With the 1960s came hotly contested, and eventually successful campaigns to create Redwood National

Steven Mather (R) and his assistant Horace Albright guided the National Park Service in its early days.

Park and Point Reyes National Seashore. During the 1970s the National Park Service established parks near the state's big cities—Golden Gate National Recreation Area on the San Francisco waterfront and Marin headlands and Santa Monica Mountains National Recreation Area, a Mediterranean ecosystem near Los Angeles. Also during that decade, Mineral King Valley was saved from a mega-ski resort development and added to Sequoia National Park. Channel Islands National Park, an archipelago offshore from Santa Barbara, was established in 1980.

During the 1980s and 1990s, major conservation battles raged in the desert. After more than two decades of wrangling, Joshua Tree and Death Valley national monuments were greatly expanded and given national park status, and the 1.6-million acre Mojave National Preserve was established under provisions of the 1994 California Desert Conservation Act.

Today, the National Park Service must address challenging questions: How best to regulate concessionaires? Should motor vehicles be banned from Yosemite Valley? How can aging park facilities cope with many years of deferred maintenance?

And the biggest issue of all: How will our parks (indeed our planet!) cope with the rapidly increasing effects of climate change?

The consequences of climate change to California's national parks is ever more apparent. In recent years, after prolonged droughts, devastating wildfires burned the Yosemite backcountry, parts of Sequoia National Park and more than half the Santa Monica Mountains National Recreation Area. Scientists have discovered that trees in Sequoia and Kings Canyon national parks endure the worst ozone levels of all national parks, in part because of their proximity to farm-belt air in the San Joaquin Valley.

California's national parklands struggle with an ever-increasing numbers of visitors. The California Office of Tourism charts visitation to national parks along with airports, hotel occupancy and other attractions such as Disneyland and Universal Studios. Yosemite is California's most-visited park with 4.5 to 5 million visitors a year, and many other parks count millions of visitors or "visitor days," per year.

What may be the saving grace of national parks is the deep-seated, multi-generational pride Americans have for their national parklands. We not only love national parks, we love the very idea of national parks. Even in an era of public mistrust toward government, national parks remain one of the most beloved institutions of American life.

National Parks have often been celebrated as America's best idea. As writer Wallace Stegner put it: "National parks are the best idea we ever had. Absolutely American, absolutely democratic, they reflect us at our best rather than our worst."

The Trails

The state of the state's national park trail system is excellent. Trailhead parking, interpretive panels and displays, as well as signage, is generally tops in the field. Backcountry junctions are usually signed and trail conditions, with a few exceptions of course, range from good to excellent.

Trail systems evolved on a park-by-park basis and it's difficult to speak in generalities about their respective origins. A good deal of Yosemite's trail system was in place before the early horseless carriages chugged into the park.

Several national parks were aided greatly by the Depression-era Civilian Conservation Corps of the 1930s. Sequoia and Pinnacles national parks, for example, have hand-built trails by the CCC that are true gems, highlighted by stonework and bridges that would no doubt be prohibitively expensive to construct today.

Scout troops, the hard-working young men and women of the California Conservation Corps and many volunteer groups are among the organizations that help park staff build and maintain trails.

The trail system in California's national parklands shares many characteristics in common with pathways overseen by other governmental bodies, and have unique qualities as well. One major difference between national parks and, for example, California's state parks, is the amount of land preserved as wilderness. A majority of Yosemite, Sequoia, Death Valley, Joshua Tree and several more parks are official federally designated wilderness. Wilderness comprises some 94 percent of Yosemite National Park, 93 percent of Death Valley National Park, and more than 80 percent of Joshua Tree National Park.

On national park maps you'll find wilderness areas delineated as simply "Wilderness." Unlike the Forest Service, the Bureau of Land Management or other wilderness stewards, the National Park Service does not name its wilderness areas.

Author John McKinney admires the sign for Yosemite's Four Mile Trail.

"Wilderness" is more than a name for a wild area. By law, a wilderness is restricted to non-motorized entry—that is to say, equestrian and foot travel. Happily, hikers do not have to share the trails with snowmobiles or mountain bikes in national park wilderness.

Because national park trails attract visitors from all over the globe, the park service makes use of international symbols on its signage, and the metric system as well. Don't be surprised if you spot trail signs with distance expressed in kilometers as well as miles and elevation noted in meters as well as feet.

The hikers you meet on a national park trail may be different from the company you keep on trails near home. California's national parks attract increasing numbers of ethnically and culturally diverse hikers of all ages, shapes and sizes, from across the nation and around the world. Once I counted ten languages on a popular trail in Yosemite! The hiking experience is much enriched by sharing the trail with hikers from literally all walks of life.

California's National Parklands

Alcatraz Island
Cabrillo National Monument
Castle Mountains National Monument
César E. Chávez National Monument
Channel Islands National Park
Death Valley National Park
Devils Postpile National Monument
Eugene O'Neill National Historic Site
Fort Point National Historic Site
Golden Gate National Recreation Area
John Muir National Historic Site
Joshua Tree National Park
Lassen Volcanic National Park
Lava Beds National Monument
Manzanar National Historic Site
Mojave National Preserve
Muir Woods National Monument
Pinnacles National Park
Point Reyes National Seashore
Port Chicago Naval Magazine National Memorial
Presidio of San Francisco
Redwood National and State Parks
Rosie the Riveter WWII Home Front National
    Historic Park
San Francisco Maritime National Historic Park
Santa Monica Mountains National Recreation Area
Sequoia and Kings Canyon National Parks
Tule Lake National Monument
Whiskeytown National Recreation Area
Yosemite National Park

The Hiker's Index

Celebrating the Scenic, Sublime and Sensational Points of Interest in California's National Parks

State with the most National Parks

California, with 9

Largest National Park in Contiguous U.S.

Death Valley with 3.3 million acres

Third Largest National Park in Contiguous U.S.

Mojave National Preserve

Foggiest Place on the West Coast

Point Reyes Lighthouse, Point Reyes National Seashore

World's Tallest Tree

A 379.7-foot high coast redwood named Hyperion in Redwood National Park

World's Largest Tree

General Sherman Tree, 275 feet tall, with a base circumference of 102 feet, growing in the Giant Forest Area of Sequoia National Park

World's Largest-In-Diameter Tree

General Grant Tree, dubbed "the nation's Christmas tree," more than 40 feet in diameter at its base, growing in Kings Canyon National Park.

Largest Elephant Seal Population on Earth

San Miguel Island, Channel Islands National Park

Highest Point in Contiguous U.S.

Mt. Whitney (14,508 feet in elevation) on the far eastern boundary of Sequoia National Park

Lowest Point in Western Hemisphere

Badwater (282 feet below sea level) in Death Valley National Park

California's Largest Island

Santa Cruz Island, Channel Islands National Park

Only Major Metropolis Bisected by a Mountain Range

Los Angeles, by the Santa Monica Mountains (National Recreation Area)

Highest Waterfall in North America

Yosemite Falls, at 2,425 feet, in Yosemite National Park

JOHN MCKINNEY

John McKinney is an award-winning writer, public speaker, and author of 30 hiking-themed books: inspiring narratives, top-selling guides, books for children.

John is particularly passionate about sharing the stories of California trails. He is the only one to have visited—and written about—all 280 California State Parks. John tells the story of his epic hike along the entire California coast in the critically acclaimed *Hiking on the Edge: Dreams, Schemes, and 1600 Miles on the California Coastal Trail.*

For 18 years John, aka The Trailmaster, wrote a weekly hiking column for the Los Angeles Times, and has hiked and enthusiastically told the story of more than 10 thousand miles of trail across California and around the world. His "Every Trail Tells a Story" series of guides highlight the very best hikes in California.

The intrepid Eagle Scout has written more than a thousand stories and opinion pieces about hiking, parklands, and our relationship with nature.

A passionate advocate for hiking and our need to reconnect with nature, John is a frequent public speaker, and shares his tales on radio, on video, and online.

JOHN MCKINNEY:
"EVERY TRAIL TELLS A STORY."

Hike On.

TheTrailmaster.com

www.ingramcontent.com/pod-product-compliance
Lightning Source LLC
Chambersburg PA
CBHW032041290426
44110CB00012B/907